THE NINTH E

VERY MUCH ENLA~~

—————————————— o,

MEMOIR

OF THE

NORTHERN IMPOSTOR;

Or PRINCE OF SWINDLERS.

Being a faithful Narrative of the ADVENTURES and DECEP-
TIONS of JAMES GEORGE SEMPLE, commonly called

MAJOR SEMPLE,

alias HARROLD. MAXWELL, GRANT, &c. &c.

With an Account of his Devices at Lord SALISBURY's, Sir
THOMAS DUNDAS's, Mr. PITT's, the MARQUIS of LANDS-
DOWN's, Baron HOMPESCH, Lord SUFFIELD, Sir SAMPSON
GIDEON, Dr. PRETTYMAN, &c. &c.

Also the various Inventions by which he obtained Goods of
different Tradefmen; and the Names of the Perfons who were
the Objects of his Depredations.

TO WHICH IS ANNEXED

His TRIAL, and SENTENCE.

LONDON:

Printed for G. KEARSLEY, No. 46, Fleet-Street. 1786.

[PRICE EIGHTEEN-PENCE.]

Entered at Stationers Hall.

Just publifhed, The Hiftory of CHARLES PRICE: with
faithful Detail of his feveral Forgeries on the Bank of England,
and various other Depredations on Society for upwards of fifty
Years.

ADVERTISEMENT.

THE artifices of that arch fwindler Major Semple, induced various perfons who have been plundered by him to contribute, without the leaft view to profit, (as appears by the bulk of the work, which is equal in quantity to a half-crown pamphlet) to print an account of the different modes by which he accomplifhed his fraudulent views; and they have employed Mr. Kearfley in Fleet-ftreet, as their publifher.

BOOKS

[v]

The following interesting Compilation has been received with the strongest Marks of Approbation, particularly among the commercial and trading Ranks of Society, for whose Accommodation it is chiefly intended. Price One Shilling.

A TABLE of TRADES, for the affistance of Parents and Guardians, and for the benefit of those young men who wish to prosper in the world.

Shewing what a Master in every profession requires as an Apprentice-Fee; what a Journeyman can earn; also, what sum is necessary to set up as Master in any Trade; with some interesting advice to Apprentices, Masters, and Parents.—*These* Tables *contain upwards of* 300 *professions.*

An Account of two new Voyages, and a Description of the Inhabitants of the Dog-star and Moon, Creatures which answer in those Planets to the Human Species: also an Engraving of each from a Drawing by the Author. Price Half-a-Crown.

The *fourth Edition*, with the above Improvements, of BARON MUNCHAUSON's ADVENTURES in RUSSIA, ICELAND, TURKEY, EGYPT, GIBRALTAR, the MEDITERRANEAN, ATLANTIC OCEAN, &c. &c.

Upon the Continent, these Adventures are at this time, more read, particularly in France, Germany, and Holland, where the Author is well known, than any production that has appeared for some years. This fourth edition, exclusive of the above improvements, is embellished with eighteen plates, whereas the French has but six; the Baron's Adventures at Gibraltar are prohibited in the French and Dutch editions, but given in full length in this English impression.

AN ABRIDGEMENT of CAPTAIN COOK's THREE VOYAGES ROUND THE WORLD. The First from 1768 to 1771; the Second, from 1772 to 1775; and the Third and Last, from 1776 to 1783. To which is added, CAPTAIN FURNEAUX's Narrative, during his separation in the second voyage. The whole containing an accurate description of all the New Discoveries, and the Inhabitants. To which is added, Captain Cook's Life, with the particulars of his death, at full length, written by Capt. King.——Each volume may be had separate, price 3s. sewed, or 3s. 6d. bound.

TO

TO

JAMES ADAIR, Esquire,

SERJEANT at LAW,

AND

RECORDER OF THE CITY OF LONDON.

SIR,

THE following pages are dedicated to you, as the humble mite of an individual, who has long been an obferver of your conduct in the high ftation to which your private virtues and public merit have fo juftly raifed you.

Your great concern for, and circumfpection in, the fecurity of property, and the freedom of the fubject, have gained you a name which will live as long as the Whig intereft of this country fhall exift.

I am,

SIR,

With the moft profound refpect,

Your obedient humble Servant,

The COMPILER.

TAB

TABLE OF CONTENTS,

a 2

His

b   Cafes

The

Mr

Mr.

Juft

Just published in a Pocket Volume,

A DESCRIPTIVE JOURNEY through the Interior Parts of GERMANY and FRANCE. With Interesting and Amusing Anecdotes. By a young ENGLISH PEER, of the highest Rank, just returned from his Travels.

Printed for G. KEARSLEY, at No. 46, Fleet-Street. *By whom also will be shortly Published,* A COLLECTION of LETTERS from the late DAVID GARRICK, Esq. to his Friends; including those which have lately appeared in the Morning Post: also several others which have never before been printed.

Kearsley has also lately printed price *Eighteen-pence,*

Ornamented with a neat Frontispiece from an original Drawing,

THE GENTLEMAN ANGLER. Containing brief and plain instructions by which the young beginner may in a short time become a perfect artist in angling for all kinds of fish. With several Observations on Rods, and Artificial Flies. Also the method of chusing the best Hair and Indian Grass; of the proper times and seasons for River and Pond Fishing; when Fish Spawn; and what Baits are chiefly to be used.

Also An APPENDIX, containing the art of Rock and Sea Fishing; and an Alphabetical Explanation of the Technical Words used in the Art of Angling.

By a GENTLEMAN of Beaconsfield, who has made it his Diversion upwards of Fourteen Years.

N. B. *This treatise on angling is quite new, and not borrowed or compiled from other productions.*

In Two Volumes,

TALES of the TWELFTH and THIRTEENTH
CENTURIES,

Among which are

The Devil and the Hermit,
The Minstrel turned out of Hell,
The Reformed Dame,
The wife that tried her Husband
The Three Theives,
The Pedlar, a comic story,
The Norman Bachelor,
The Tradesmen and the Clown,
The Knight and the Trap-door,
The Three Hunch-back Minstrels,
The Parsons's Cow,
The Woman that made twice the circuit of the
 Church,
The Woman that ensnared a Priest, a Provost,
 and a Ranger,
The Queen that killed her Seneschal,
The Knight that confessed his Wife,
The Wife of Orleans,
The Parson's Legacy,
The Citizen of Abeville,
The Three Beggars of Compeigne,

And several others which cannot be noticed in the
 limits of this advertisement.

Price Six Shillings sewed.

⁂ *Upon these tales the principal part of our ro-
mances and dramatic pieces have been founded.*

MEMOIRS.

MEMOIRS

OF THE

NORRHERN IMPOSTOR.

A S this is the ninth time of printing thefe
Memoirs, it is hoped they will anfwer the
intention of publication, viz. to guard the unwary, againft the depredations of common cheats.
It is neither a new nor a fingular obfervation,
that every century hath produced a Genius,
and every country an Hero. There is no neceffity to have recourfe to the annals of the ancients,
or to the multiplied inftances of modern hiftory
to juftify the affertion. France has had her Char-
latan, and her Comteffe de la Motte. Jonathan
Wild, and Mrs. Margaretta Matilda Sophia Ca-
roline Rudd, may fafely difpute the laurel with
the Gallic Hero and Heroine : but Britain, the
queen of ifles, feems to be the natural foil for the
cultivation of fuch genius and heroifm.

A few years, however, have determined to
whom the laurel wreath is due. We have had
Minifters of the Church of England executed
for forgery and murder, and a Methodift Prea-
cher, in holy orders, hanged for abufing
young children, to whom he was fchool-mafter.
Lawyers and Contractors have kept perjury in
countenance ; and the GREAT CHARLES PRICE,
juftly ftiled *The* SOCIAL MONSTER, rufhed into

B   the

the prefence of his Maker, rather than have his genius recorded in the Ordinary's Calendar of Newgate Heroes.

The progrefs of heroifm has led us into thefe obfervations. They prove, that a very few years have eclipfed the tranfactions of ages, and that England can boaft of more renowned exploits in that fhort period of time, than ever were fignalized throughout all Europe during the laft century.

It was the reflection of a great lawyer, that the laws of this country were made to bind a *bold* and *daring* race of people. In his days, the refinements of modern villainy were unknown, and therefore unpractifed. The name of SWINDLER, a creature begot between Downright Robbery and Dame Forgery, was unheard of.

It is alfo an eftablifhed truth, that the powers of legiflation can never keep pace with inventive knavery, the natural depravity of mankind baffling every attempt to deter it. The efforts of moral writers have been equally fuccefslefs to reftrain the vicious part of it from unprincipled difhonefty.—Thus whilft the abfurdity of our penal ftatutes have opened doors of invitation to ingenious chicanery, the fcandalous and contemptible artifices of dirty pettifogging attornies, and Old Bailey bar-orators, have given a loofe and encouragement to every fpecies of fraud and impofition.

T

To inftance this—An act of parliament was made, which decreed it a capital offence to fteal horfes, mares, or geldings. The firft man who was ever tried upon that act, pleaded the *fingular number*.——As he had only ftolen *a horfe*, he was —acquitted.—It was a penal ftatute, and not to be *liberally* conftrued.—The *text* was to be ftrictly adhered to.

To prevent the receiving of ftolen goods, knowing them to have been ftolen, in the enumeration of the articles, watches were omitted. They are held not to come under the defcription of goods, wares, or merchandize : a receiver of ftolen goods may therefore purchafe as many watches as he pleafes, of whom he pleafes, and at what price he thinks proper.

In the act againft dog-ftealing, the magiftrate has a power to fine, imprifon, and order the immediate correction of the houfe. After conviction, and when the culprit's back has been flead, he may, by a very wife provifion in that act, appeal to the quarter feffions to reverfe the flogging !

Turnips might have been ftolen with impunity, for they were omitted in the act that made it felony to fteal any thing elfe out of gardens, fields, &c. &c. in confequence of which a new act was made.

It is well known alfo, that a man may fet fire to his *own* houfe, and not be punifhable by any ftatute law.

Thefe

These preposterous absurdities and scandalous technical omissions, call loudly for the interposition and inspection of the Twelve Judges whenever a penal statute is framed. The various and curious labyrinths of the laws would then be reduced into a plain and easy road, nor would the incorrigible rogue find a *stimulus* from their subtle and encouraging constructions,

The only argument that ever was advanced against consulting the Judges on these occasions is, that they are servants and officers of the crown, *durante bene placitur*, and therefore ought never to interfere in framing laws, where the preservation of his Majesty's crown and dignity is concerned, as they may be supposed to be partial to their royal master. To answer this flimsy argument is neither our business or design at present.

But though these legal inaccuracies and curious distinctions operate, in one sense, to the great disadvantages of the community, yet in another, they afford the most pleasing satisfaction, by protecting the life, liberty, and property of Englishmen. For if laws are ever to be construed otherwise than written, a partial and severe Judge, or a packed and corrupt Jury, might stretch the arm of resentment, either to serve their own private animosities, or to favour the designing views of an arbitrary and profligate administration,

The

The late Sir John Fielding, whose unwearied endeavours to check the progress of all sorts of vice, must make his name remembered with high respect, discovered, in his official capacity, the very great misfortune of what we now complain. —He daily experienced the triumph of villainy, especially in that line which is now the subject of this performance. He applied to parliament, and with much difficulty he procured an act for the better prevention of frauds, (the 30th of Geo. II.) commonly called *Fielding's Act*, which secures the property of tradesmen from the pernicious arts of those public robbers, usually denominated SWIND-LERS; for that which was then deemed but a debt, is now determined to be a felony.

To that magistrate, therefore, are the public indebted for the detection of that delinquent, whose extraordinary feats of ingenuity, have struck so much alarm and terror throughout the private as well as mercantile line of life.—At the same time justice obliges us to add, that the exertions of Mr. Feltham, co-operating with the spirit of that act, have carried into effect an event that has for many years been most devoutly wished.

We must observe also, that although cultivated knavery is generally imputed to the southern inhabitants of this island, yet the perfection of the science was reserved for a native of North Britain.

After

After this exordium we proceed to our fub. ject.

James George Semple was born about the year 1750, at Irvine, in the fhire of Ayr, and is now about thirty-fix years of age. He is the fon of a Mr. James Semple, who was once a furveyor in the cuftom-houfe at Scotland ; who is alfo living, but from fome occafion or other, has *refigned* his place.

We were the more particular in this circum-ftance, not only as it fatisfies our readers of the birth and parentage of our Hero, but alfo, as it leads to a circumftance that could not poffibly be omitted, efpecially in a narrative of fuch great actions as we mean to tranfmit to pofterity.

In the year 1547, the title of Lord Vifcount Lyfle, of the kingdom of Scotland became *extinct* ; The reader may be affured it was not *attainted*. There is no record whatever of its difaffection to government, and therefore may be juftly ftiled as loyal a family as any that North Britain can boaft.

The dormancy of this title has continued two hundred and thirty-nine years. The father of our Hero, James Semple, we hear has lately laid claim to it. We mention this to fhew that there is ftrong fuppofition of the dregs of very rich blood run-ring in the veins of James George Semple. It alfo not only adds an importance and dignity to

his

his character, but interests the reader a little more in his fate. To have a Hero the defcendant of a long line of anceftry, is one great effort of modern, tragedy; but without fearching the hiftories of the Greeks and Romans, or rummaging the Ottoman traditions, we have *ipfo fatto*, fuch. an interefting character from the highlands of Scotland. The phœnix of the family of Lyfle.

His education was at the place of his nativity, Irvine; and it would be fuperfluous to add, that he was foon made converfant in Latin and Greek. In thofe exercifes he had no competitor; his juvenile abilities foon diftinguifhed themfelves, and kept his fchool-fellows at an humble diftance. We may add too, that as his years increafed, fome other eminent proficiencies kept them at a ftill greater. To be plain, moft of the parents of the fcholars of Irvine were under the neceffity of directing their children not to affociate with James George Semple.

As he grew towards manhood, an elegant figure, a perfon exceeding well made, and a genteel deportment gave him a pre-eminency in point of attraction. To thefe ornaments were added an underftanding capable of every improvement, and an affability of temper, fo confonant to *the things that be*, that he was a moft engaging companion, wherever he could introduce himfelf.

Thefe

These qualifications, notwithstanding the others we just hinted at, whilst they procured him the envy and dislike of the male part of the creation, made him ample amends by the favour and esteem in which he was held by the females of all ranks ages and conditions.

One observation arises here. These tinsel attractions, and these flattering partialities of the ladies, are the rocks on which our youth have too frequently split. They are the Scylla and Charybdis of every young man, whose knowledge is like a whipt syllabub, and whose vanity leads him to suppose himself something, when in truth and in fact they reduce him to a mere non-entity. One deformed sensible good man, is of more service to society than, thousand gay superficial flutterers, with fine figures, even tho' they should be vulgarly honest. Ex. Gr.

To the partiality of the sex, we hear Mr. Semple was indebted for his abdication of Irvine; but we wish not to wound the vitals of suffering credulity in one sex, by exposing the iniquitous arts of the other; or to hang up the name of a lady, when we wish only to delineate the character of James George Semple. In order to improve his natural advantages, he was sent, as we are informed, to the college at Edinburgh, and intended for the Kirk, to which profession he was originally bred. He had not, however, been long there, before he gave ample proofs, that the study of

religion

religion was not calculated for a perſon of his lively diſpoſition and gay turn of mind. The ſtudy of phyſic was then propoſed to him, but that ſcilence was too abſtruſe and technical to attract his attention. Law ſeemed to be his favorite amuſement at college, and his father, determined to let his ſon take what courſe of ſtudy he pleaſed, agreed he ſhould become a lawyer, no doubt with a view to prevent his becoming a rogue.

This reminds us of a repartee made uſe of by the magiſtrate whoſe name we have already mentioned. A fellow who made it a practice to pay fixpence for a baſon of ſoup at various coffee-houſes, and ſteal at the ſame time a ſilver table ſpoon, was at laſt detected. Sir John Fielding aſked him what he was? To which the gentleman replied, "I belong to the Law, Sir." "The Law! pſhaw! damme! that's impoſſible," ſaid Sir John, "if you did you would have ſtolen the *baſon* too."

How long he continued his ſtudies there we are not thoroughly acquainted with, but we are informed that it is near nine years ſince his name was firſt enrolled on the liſts in the black book of Bow-ſtreet, under the title CHEVALIERS DES INDUSTRIE. From this account we may draw a tolerable calculation that he had not been a conſiderable time in London, before he recommended himſelf to the notice and attention of the police.

C   Having

Having thus traced Mr. Semple's nativity and education, we beg leave to ſay a little more reſpecting his firſt introduction into this great metropolis, where abilities like his have a wide field to diſplay themſelves in, and where induſtry never can be in want of a guinea.

The ſituation of Mr. Semple's father had been naturally ſuch, as to bring him to the knowledge of a certain gentleman, who was intimate with a Scotch merchant, who was acquainted with an attorney, or rather writer at Edinburgh, who was the friend of a gentleman who was very well acquainted with one of the lords of Trade, now one of the lords of his Majeſty's Bed-chamber, who was an intimate friend of one of the directors of the Eaſt India Company.

Now it ſo happened, that there was ſuch a good underſtanding between that certain gentleman, that Scotch merchant, and the lawyer, who tranſacted the buſineſs of the ſaid lord, that the writer, upon the firſt application, declared that young Semple *ſhould* have a place in the Eaſt India Company's ſervice abroad.

Upon this abſolute promiſe from ſuch a great man, the elder Semple equipped James George with all proper materials for ſuch a journey to the Eaſt ; not forgetting the requiſites neceſſary to convey him to London, where he ſuppoſed he had

nothing

nothing to do but to call on the chairman of that company and receive his appoinment.

Notwithftanding, however, that abfolute pro-mife, young Semple found fome little difficulty in obtaining it; and, being a *bon vivant*, he ex-haufted his refources with a facility that foon com-pelled him to have recourfe to the old man for a frefh fupply, under the pretence of the neceffary extra-vagance he was compelled to live at in London.

Having obtained a fupply, he diffipated that with as much fpeed as he had done his for-mer finances; and whilft his applications at the Eaft-India Houfe, and attendance there, fhould have been renewed with hourly vigour, his only ftudy was to adorn his fweet perfon, and com-mence fine gentleman. The lazinefs of his life foon led him into company, capable of complet-ing his utmoft wifhes, and all ideas of ventur-ing fo dangerous a voyage and climate were as foon exploded.

Gay life and gay company fpeedily brought on unhappy projects to fupport it. It was to this in-advertent ftep in the elder Semple, of intrufting his fon as his own mafter in a town, where the utmoft refolution and fortitude are too often in-effectual fecurity againft vice and debauchery, that the younger Semple owes his ruin. It was more highly criminal in him, as he knew the natu-ral bent of his fon's inclinations. Let us pity,

there-

therefore, whilſt we condemn; though at the ſame time, the inadvertence of a father is no apology for the immoralities of a ſon.

In the purſuit of his pleaſure, it was a little unfortunate for a family of great character and reſpect in Devonſhire, the G———ts, that he became their acquaintance. To the daughter of it, it was a moſt irreparable misfortune. She was married to him, and it was not long before Mr. Semple gave very convincing proofs how his noble blood inſpired him to maintain, unſullied, the honour and dignity of the houſe of Lyſle.

After he had married into the before-mentioned family, and his way of life had ſo diſguſted the lady's parents, that they never would conſent to ſee him, they offered to ſettle upon her 200l. per ann. if ſhe would quit her huſband. But ſuch is the prevalence of paſſion in the female part of the creation, that they are not only blind to their own intereſts, but to the defects and vices of him, who, unhappily, chances to be the God of their idolatry.

Mrs. Semple then refuſed the offer; but at length, wearied with habitual enormities, ſhe has conſented to remove herſelf entirely out of his reach. Not thinking herſelf ſafe in England, where ſhe could be peſtered with his viſits and applications, ſhe wiſely choſe to retire to a ſpot where the ſingularity of his adventures has forecloſed

all

all ideas of difturbance. She is now at Calais; where Mr. Semple, for a long time paft, has not ventured to make his appearance, and for a reafon which to him was a very formidable one. He had already experienced the pleafures of three years imprifonment in Calais gaol; and, not defirous of revifiting his old habitation, very wifely omitted that fea-port in his latter vifits to the continent.

The univerfity of Oxford alfo has had the honour of Mr. Semple's being a member of their county gaol for debt; where he remained only five days, and was then matriculated.

We have it alfo from good authority, that he frequented every place of fafhionable amufement, and was received by fome families of diftinction as a vifitor, and as a gentleman of birth and character, whofe father was claiming an extinct title.

Tell me your company and I'll tell you the man, is a very old faying. How far it was verified by Mr. Semple, the loweft capacity can judge. As there was no company in life which he had not entered into, from the plain gentleman up to the reprefentative of Majefty, fo had he contracted their principles, he muft with his qualifications, have been an ornament to fociety; but as Shakefpeare fays, *Tow'ring ambition which over-vaulteth itfelf,* was the fource of all his misfortunes. He *would* keep great company, which muft be attended with a great expence; and in order to furnifh himfelf

with

with the means of supporting it, he was compelled
to have recourse to great actions.

It was from this connection however, he luckily
obtained a recommendation to quit his native
country. The Ruffian service was propofed and
embraced. The G——t family knew how very
fortunate it might turn out for, them, and they
were happy to hit on any expedient which promifed a reftoration of their former felicity. Mr.
Semple, therefore, departed for the dominions of
the Emprefs, equipped with thofe requifites, which
were accepted with as much fatisfaction on one
fide, as they were beftowed with good will on the
other.

Though it will be neceffary here to ftate that
Mrs. Semple is the God-daughter of the celebrated
Dutchefs of Kingfton; yet it need fcarcely be told
that that great lady is a very great favourite with
the ftill greater Emprefs of Ruffia, at which court
the firft great lady now refides.

To conceive that J. G. Semple would let flip fo
favourable an opportunity of improving his fortunes,
would be but paying a very bad compliment to
his penetration. As he knew the alliance, fo he
knew well how to introduce himfelf. Mr. Semple
was a fine man, the lady had been a fine woman,
and is ftill a great wit; fhe received him with
hofpitality, and promifed to introduce him to the
Emprefs. The promife of a court lady was never
yet

yet violated. Mr. Semple was introduced, and promifed promotion.

But ftrange was the revolution in the affairs of Mr. Semple.—A fomething, a deftiny which we all are liable to, threw a ftumbling block in his way.—The Dutchefs withdrew her favours, the Emprefs recanted her promife, and Mr. Semple decamped without waiting for the expected promotion.

The great actions that were the fpring of this event are recorded in page 95 of thefe Memoirs.

But although we are not at a lofs for fo important a circumftance in the life of Mr. Semple; yet we have the pleafure of recording here one fmall fpecimen of his ingenuity ere we bring him out of a country which was fo unfortunate in his lofs. He *borrowed* the paffport of the king's meffenger, then on his road to England, and by quitting the character of a gentleman, and affuming that which the contents of the paffport afforded him, he got fafe into Germany, where he talked in the language of the fellow upon Highgate-hill, who bid the Lord Mayor of London kifs-his ———.

At Cologne he diftinguifhed himfelf in a manner no ways derogatory to that affurance which had already made him pretty confpicuous in England and Ruffia. Whether the incident we are going to relate happened at this, or at a fubfequent period,

period, we are not certain; be the time when it will, it makes but a very little difference to the reader. It is a fact, and therefore the order of time totally immaterial.

Baron Hompefch, a German nobleman, was refident at Cologne, when Mr. Semple arrived there, by which the latter had an opportunity of exercifing thofe wits which feemed to have been his only fupport for fome years. He addreffed himfelf to the Baron with all the politenefs he was capable of, and that was no fmall portion. He ftiled himfelf a Major in his Britannic Majefty's fervice, defcribed himfelf of a noble family in Scotland, and boafted his great intimacy with the firft of the Englifh nobility; concluding with his relationfhip to the lady who had given him fo kind a reception at the Court of Peterfburgh.

Having thus ftated his confequence, he then opened his misfortunes.—He had been fo unhappy, he faid, as to kill two Englifh gentlemen, one at London, the other at Bath, in a duel. From his confequence and misfortunes, he then began to difplay his legal abilities.—The laws of England, he faid, were very fevere on the laws of honour, and cruelly deemed that a murder, which the laws of other countries took no cognizance of, and by this cruelty he was compelled to fly for fafety to a foreign country.—His mind was exceedingly diftreffed, but he was much more fo by the fitua-

tion

tion in which his pecuniary affairs then stood; and both those causes emboldened him to seek the support of a nobleman, whose soul was ever awake to the sensations of humanity, particularly when a gentleman and a distressed officer put in his plea to those feelings.

His manner, his appearance, his language, operated effectually on the Baron. The eye of pity was thrown on so unhappy and so unfortunate a case. The Baron's purse bestowed the most liberal relief, and his house afforded a most comfortable asylum. The Baron's friendship and services kept pace with the Major's misfortunes, and he promised to use all his interest to get him restored to his native country.

But this extension of friendship was not all that the Major prevailed on the Baron to exert—Mr. Semple wished to return to England with his Majesty's promise of a pardon in case of conviction; for, added he, "As a gentleman and a man of honour, I must surrender myself up to the laws of the land, and take my trial for the murders."

The Baron, who perhaps better understood the constitution of Germany, and some other northern nations than that of England, and knew that whilst the laws of the land was tying a halter round a man's neck, the monarch was tying round the ribband of some honorary order round his shoulders, readily consented to this request, and assured Mr.

D

Semple,

Semple, he would use all his influence to procure the King's previous pardon, as soon as ever he should arrive in England, which would be in the space of two or three months.

To relieve the reader from any suspence which he may be thrown into, by Mr. Semple's narrative of duels he never fought, and of men he never killed, we must let him into a secret which it is not impossible he may have already discovered. The whole tale was an artful deception, trumped up for the mere purpose of living on the Baron's bounty as a man of consequence and fashion, which was always the ambition of James George Semple, Esq. Besides, as he knew that his happy effrontery, and external appearance could support the character, so he knew that the only method of carrying his plan into execution, was to put himself upon a level with the Baron. We may be liberal to the poor and base born ; but effectual relief and friendship are only extended to our equals.

In this noble state did Major Semple live at Cologne till the time of the Baron's departure for England, when the Major accompanied him, not in his suite, but as a friend and companion. On their arrival, the Baron mentioned the case to some of his Majesty's ministers ; by whom he was informed, that the request was impossible to be granted, as all offences here were punished or par-

doned

doned according to the merits of the case, and the favourable or aggravating circumstances attending it.

Soon after the Baron's arrival it happened that Count Hompesch, the Baron's son, came from Germany to England with dispatches. After having negotiated his business, he was preparing to return; when the Baron advised Major Semple to accompany him, and he should have his recommendations there. This was readily agreed to, but a little delay proposed, in order to settle his private affairs in England. The Count would have been happy in the Major's company, but submitted to the mortification of sailing without him. His luggage, however, was large, and as it could not be all got together by the time, especially as he purchased many valuable English articles, the Major kindly took charge of the remainder, which by some damn'd accident or other on the road, never got over to Cologne, although as we are informed, it was worth between four and five hundred pounds. It is hardly worth our notice to observe, that in a visit to Mr. Richardson, sugar-baker, of Stamford-street, over Black-fryar's bridge, with the baron, he borrowed five shillings of Mr. Richardson's maid servant for want of change to pay a coach, and forgot to return it.

What became of Mr. Semple immediately after this loss, we are not positive, but we find him at

Dieppe,

Dieppe, in about a year afterwards, hiring an English fishing-smack, there being no packet-boat, for
the exprefs purpofe of bringing over difpatches to
government here, as he declared. For this con-
veyance he agreed to give fourteen guineas. When
he arrived at Harwich, not having cafh about him
to pay it, and being alfo in want of money to pay
the chaife to town, as he told the man, he borrowed
fix guineas of him (Mr. Thomas Welfh, living
at No. 7, Gun-alley, Wapping, with whom Mr.
Semple travelled over the ocean in the name and
defcription of Colonel Crawford.

But a fingular inftance of his ingenuity ought
not to efcape us. It exhibits his addrefs, and the
fertility of his genius too powerfully to be fup-
preffed.

He applied to Mr. Lovett, ftable-keeper and
hackney-man, of Stratton Street, Piccadilly, in
order to fend an exprefs down to Lord Salifbury,
at Hatfield. The exprefs was fent, and contained
an account of a near relation of her ladyfhip's and
his own alfo, who, Mr. Semple faid, was arrefted
for three hundred pounds, mentioning the perfon's
name, and that fixty or eighty guineas would com-
promife the affair. This letter, by the exprefs,
was delivered to his Lordfhip, as he was riding
near the houfe, but to which his Lordfhip returned
this verbal anfwer, " *That he knew of no fuch perfon,
or relation, and therefore there was no anfwer.*"

The

The obvious meaning of this exprefs was, firft to make himfelf appear a perfon of confequence and fafhion by his connections; and, fecondly, upon the ftrength of it, to get credit of Mr. Lovett. The fchemo had its effect. He ran a few pounds into Mr. Lovett's debt ; who, having fome little knowledge of the world, began to fufpect the Major, and then put a *curb* to his credit.

Many and vain were his applications after Mr. Semple for payment. Fortunately he obferved him one Day in a hackney coach, and the Major, in his turn, difcovered Mr. Lovett. He kept himfelf like an hair in his form, at the bottom of the coach, whence Mr. Lovett ftarted him by opening the coach door.---Pleas, apologies, and excufes, flowed as freely as the Thames at a fpring tide.--- His honour and his Maker he offered as bail for the performance of his promifes, but Mr. Lovett would neither take the fecurity, nor part with his game ; and fwore, wherever the coach went, thither he would go alfo.

When the Major found that there was no getting rid of his companion, he declared it was hard that he fhould be compelled to apply perfonally to his agents for a few pounds ; but as neceffity had no law, if Mr. Lovett would accompany him to Meffrs. Cox and Mair's, in Craig's-Court, Charing-Crofs, he would pay him.

There

There is no doubt but Mr. Lovett readily consented to the proposal.—They drove to Craig's Court, where he got out of the coach; and as Mr. Lovett well knew it was no thoroughfare, he continued at the corner of the court, and saw him go into Messrs. Cox and Mair's.

After waiting an hour he began to grow impatient. He enquired at the agents for Major Semple: they knew no such man: but the servant maid informed him, that a gentleman, about an hour ago had been there, and told her he was pursued by bailiffs, and begged her to let him escape through the house by the back door into Scotland-yard, which, out of compassion she had done. By this double Mr. Lovett lost his game, and never got scent again.

- -But the circle of his ingenuities were not limited to Barons, Counts, Watermen, and Hackney-coachmen; the Keepers of Coffee-houses and Hotels experienced their pleasant effects likewise.

He frequented Wood's hotel, under Covent-Garden Piazza; and although Mr. Wood has, to our knowledge, too much good sense to be amused by the inventive genius of plausible pretenders, when their artillery is levelled at the purse, yet Major Semple proved an over-match for Mr. Wood's general prudence.

The Major came there one day, and desired to know for how many such a gentleman, (the reader

must

must excuse our naming him) had ordered dinner?
—Mr. Wood replied, " He had no orders."
—Good God! said the Major, Dick is a sad dog!
How neglectful! Why, Wood, several of us a-
greed last night to dine with you to-day at seven
shillings and sixpence a head, exclusive of wines.
—Get dinner ready at five o'clock for a dozen.
Mr. Wood was retiring to give orders, when the
Major called him back:—Here, hark ye, Wood,
said he, damme if I am not come out and left my
purse on the table:—Lend me six guineas. Mr.
Wood lent the money, the Major departed, an ele-
gant dinner was dressed, but neither that sad dog,
Dick, nor any of his party, came to partake of it.

We trace him likewise to a lodging at Knights-
bridge with a Mr. Sadgrove, a hair-dresser there,
in the name of Major Harrold: To Mr. Sadgrove's he brought with him an elderly gentleman, whom he was pleased to stile his father, and
to dignify with the appellation of Lord Lysle.—
When Mr. Sadgrove apologised for the inconve-
nience he should be under in accommodating a
nobleman—Pshaw, said the Major, put him into
my bed, and make up one any how for me.—
Thus were the nobleman and his son accommodated, till Mr. Sadgrove began to trouble his
lodgers for some of those reasons which make all
inconveniencies trifling to the person who submits
to them.

But

But as Major Harrold was at a lofs for that kind of eloquence, and as fome few neighbouring tradefmen applied for the fame fort of oratory, Mr. Sadgrove's lodgings began to be thought too far from town, and confequently the Major re-moved, but without giving legal notice thereof.

Many were the fearches Mr. Sadgrove made to make him fpeak properly, but they were fruitlefs. Having at laft traced Major Harrold, Mr. Sadgrove received from him the following curious letter :

Mr. Sadgrove,

I received yefterday from the gentleman who is with me, a letter which you meant for me, but which he opened owing to the addrefs. I affure you that upon my word that before Thurfday next I will pay you the money I remain in your debt; but *I muft beg you will not mention that I am in town to any body.* I will call myfelf at your houfe and pay you. If I promife you fooner I may not be able to keep my word, but then I affure you I will not *faill*, but *I beg you will not mention having feen me.* Friday afternoon.

P. S. I again affure you that I will not *faill* on Thurfday to pay you—*only don't mention that you have feen me.*

Directed to Mr. Sadgrove, Hair-Dreffer, No. 10, Gloucefter-Row, Knightfbridge.

The

The reason of the Major's defiring fecrecy is too apparent to need explanation.—But to do him all poffible juftice, we muft add, that he declined putting Sadgrove to any expence about the letter, as Major Harold paid the porter, and indorfed it fo.

Having done him that piece of juftice, truth obliges us to own, that a German fervant who was with him there, [Peter Frankin] he difpatched to Oftend under pretence of preparing lodgings for him there, and who is now at Duffeldorf; having firft in cafh borrowed, and wages, ftood indebted to the poor fellow near upon twenty pounds.

Nor was he lefs active, during his ftay at Knightf-bridge, among hackney coachmen, than he had been with Mr. Lovett. Under pretence of want-ing change, he borrowed of feveral the paltry fums of ten, of twelve, and fifteen fhillings, which he never returned. If, therefore, we compare them and the former circumftance together, we are afraid that we muft conclude, that Major Harrold paid Mr. Sadgrove out of a principle of fear, and that he ftands ftill indebted to Peter Frankin, from the principle of never having meant to pay him at all.

We muft confefs, however, that Mr. Sadgrove's luck was rather fingular. Mr. Dalby, of New-Bond-Street, was not quite fo fortunate. By the means of a fine carriage, and a fine infinuating tongue, he not only got trifles to the amount of fix or feven pounds, but likewife obtained ten pounds in cafh.

He did indeed, when he purchafed the goods of Mr. Dalby, offer two guineas in part, which he faid was all the cafh he had about him; but then to take two guineas in part of fix from a gen-

E   tleman

tleman of Major Semple's appearance, Mr. Dalby was afraid might have been confidered as ungenteel, and perhaps conftrued into an affront: He therefore politely gave him credit for the whole, and without fcruple lent the Major ten pounds more to it.

To Mr. Gladwell, wine-merchant, No. 52, Piccadilly, he introduced himfelf as Major Semple, and faid, he came recommended by the Earl of Kerry.—The purport of the vifit to Mr. Gladwell was to purchafe fome wines, particularly Tent, of which he underftood that Mr. Gladwell had fome, that was very curious, as a prefent for Lady Coventry, who was moft exceedingly fond of Tent wine.—A quantity to a confiderable amount was agreed on, and a carter fent in the afternoon to fetch it away; who, on Mr. Gladwell's enquiring, told him, that he had lived with the Major fifteen years, and he was a very worthy honeft Gentleman.—The wines were packed up and fent, and the Major came in a day or two to give a fecond order; but Mr. Gladwell having, from fome little enquiry, learnt what was fufficiently fatisfactory to him, declined executing it.

In the name of Major Campbell he alfo paid a vifit to Mr. Johnfon, wine-merchant, of Bruton-Place, and had the pleafure of drinking that Gentleman's health in fome very fine-flavoured Claret and Madeira.

But though his operations were daily directed againft tradefmen, yet the nobility likewife were peftered with his impertinent affiduities.

He frequently wrote letters to Lord Salifbury, and Sir Thomas Dundas, in Arlington-ftreet, in the name of Major Campbell, till directions were
given

given by his Lordſhip and Sir Thomas, neither to admit or receive a letter from him. Defeated thus, he applied to the porter of the latter for the 'loan' of half-a-guinea, to pay for the carriage of ſome goods which were in Piccadilly, brought to town by a ſtage-waggon, and which he could not ſend home directly, as he had left his purſe on the table,—*Tel maître, tel valet*—the party-coloured tribe ape their maſters, and the porter in this caſe profited by 'following the Baronet's example.

But though thus defeated at Lord Saliſbury's and Sir Thomas Dundas's, his frequent viſits there were the occaſion of making him ſome trifling amends in the ſame ſtreet.—Greenwood and Hud-ſon, ſeedſmen, at the corner of it, from ſeeing his frequent viſits at both houſes, made no ſcruple of giving him credit, in the name of Major George, for ſeveral pounds worth of flower ſeeds, &c. From which we may draw this obſervation, that James George Semple was like a rabbit in a warren, no ſooner out of one hole than he was in at another.

Nor were his dexterities leſs practiſed upon the publican than the Peer.—Mr. Henderſon, of the Roſe and Crown public-houſe, in the Haymarket, had lived ſervant with a Captain Cunningham, of the Royals; which, by ſome means or other, Mr. Semple was acquainted with.—He came there-fore one day in a coach to Mr. Henderſon, ſaying he was ſent by Captain Cunningham to borrow a guinea, and called himſelf Captain Maxwell. The guinea was lent, 'and alſo two ſhillings to pay for the coach. Had he upon that occaſion aſked for ten, he might as eaſily have obtained it.

Another guinea he obtained of Mr. Carter riding-maſter, of Chapel-ſtreet, Groſvenor-ſquare,

by

by pretending that officers had been after him to arreſt him, and he wanted to eſcape in a coach.

The ſame ſpecimen of his abilities, Mr. Lancaſter, coachmaker, of Theobald's-Road, experienced, and under the ſame pretence, but in the name of Major Stewart.

Having taken a lodging at Mr. Lock's, No. 17, Upper Mary-le-Bone-ſtreet, where he did not go by any name but that of the Major, Mr. Lock in a ſhort time diſcovered who his lodger was, and accoſted him with a How do you do, Major Semple? The Major moved off rather precipitately, leaving a trunk with a few contents behind him, which juſt indemnified Mr. Lock. But, as Major Semple had, ſoon after that march, the honour of making a figure in a public news-paper, we ſhould neither do our Readers nor the Major juſtice, to let ſlip ſo favourable an opportunity of laying before them the following ſmall notice which chance has luckily thrown into our hands.

" If J. G. Semple, who left his lodgings at
" Daniel Lock's, No. 17, Upper Marybone-
" ſtreet, near Portland-Chapel, does not fetch the
" trunk away which he left there, in 14 days from
" this date, the ſame will be appraiſed and ſold.

" Witneſs my hand,   DANIEL LOCK."
" May 29, 1786."

It was impoſſible for us not to avail ourſelves of ſo authentic a document, however trifling; but the more material inſtances of his abilities, which, like the ſplendour of an Eaſtern Bulſe, annihilates the faint radiance of a Briſtol ſtone, totally eclipſe all ſuch petty efforts of occaſional genius.

To Mr. Wetton, of Bruton-ſtreet, confectioner, he gave a large order for confectionary, which was not executed; but though Mr. Semple failed in that, he was accommodated with half-a-dozen pots of ſweetmeats gratis.

The Reader, no doubt, has already ſeen that no ſituation in life was too high or too low for Mr. Semple to practiſe upon. From Baron Hompeſch to hackney-coachmen, mankind were alike to him; nay, a poor fellow of the name of Lucas, a porter at the Temple-gate, he conde-ſcended to borrow ſix ſhillings of to pay a hack-ney-coachman, under the pretence of having no-thing but Bank notes and bills about him.

Nor was Mr. M'Kenzie, of the Rhedarium, Park-lane, more guarded againſt his enterpriſes. Of him he obtained a carriage, and the hire of ſeveral, by the name of Major Winter. Fortune, however, ſtood M'Kenzie's friend. The Major having offered it for ſale to Mr. Careleſs, maſter of the White-Hart, at Watford, who happened to know the carriage and owner, he ſent to Mr. M'Kenzie, who came down to Watford, and iſſued out a *capias* againſt the Major, commonly known by the name of the Brewer's Ejectment Writ:—The Brewer's Ejectment Writ is this; when publicans don't pay, or are ſuſpected of decamping, or for any other *reaſonable cauſe*, the Brewer ſends his men, horſes, and drays, very legally breaks open the cellar-door, and very coolly draws away every beer butt therein. Mr. M'Kenzie, therefore, wiſely took the ſame method; he ſent his men and horſes, and brought the carriage back to the Rhedarium.

But

But although Mr. M'Kenzie was so far fortunate, yet he and Mr. Careless were joint-sufferers by letting horses and carriages out for the Major's use.

Mr. Lycett, of Whitechapel, a coach-maker, was, however, not quite so lucky as Mr. M'Kenzie:—Mr. James George Semple, in the name of J. G. Harrold, of the Hague, obtained of him a carriage to use for a fortnight; for which the Major was to pay Mr. Lycett 5s. per day. The Major sent a pair of horses, which brought it away; and he forgot ever after to pay for the use of, or to return the carriage. Nay, the Major even forgot his way to Whitechapel. How far this little ingenuity comes under the statute of felonies, will be seen hereafter; as the Major was tried for it.[*]

Mr. Greenfill, silversmith, in the Strand, also experienced the address and dexterity of this singular genius. The Major had, by his usual dexterity, insinuated himself into the opinion of a Gentleman, an Officer in his Majesty's service, a man of honour and honesty, to mention whose name would be cruel as well as indelicate. His own feelings at having been so imposed on, and which was the cause of several tradesmen giving credit to James George Semple, is a circumstance of sufficient mortification, without any additional aggravation of ours.—At Mr. Greenfill's they tossed up for some buckles; and in a few days after, on the strength of his having been in that Gentleman's company, Mr. Greenfill gave him credit for a few pounds worth of silver goods in the name of Major Cunningham. Luckily he obtained no more. Had he desired it, Mr. Green-fill

---

[*] See the Trial, pages 105 to 116.

fill would readily have credited him for fifty or an hundred pounds.

One general obfervation we beg leave to make. Wherever Mr. Semple attempted to obtain, or was fuccefsful in obtaining either money or goods, the impofition was founded on his real or pretended knowledge of fome refpectable character who he knew was acquainted with, or was a cuftomer to, the perfon he applied to, either to borrow cafh, or take up goods upon credit.— This artifice was feconded by the deception of his own perfonal appearance, which, added to the natural plaufibility of his language, was as fpecious and as alluring as the Grand Deceiver's, who, by the *honey-dew* of his tongue, and, as Voltaire fays, by the length of a fhining tail, impofed on the natural credulity of the firft frail fair. This will, once for all, account for his fuccefs in that line of Swindling, at which he was fo complete an adept, and in fome meafure apologize for the credulity of thofe who have been fufferers through his adroitnefs.

As explanatory of this, we give the following fact :

He lately, and which the Reader will fee, with an affurance equal to his artifice, applied himfelf to Mr. Hankey, of Upper Harley-ftreet, Cavendifh-fquare, although a total ftranger, and requefted the fum of feventeen or eighteen guineas, which he faid he was much in need of, to affift a brother Officer, who was then in cuftody for debt. To take off a little of the edge of a furprife which fuch a ftrange importunity might naturally occafion, he added, that he was a Major in his Majefty's fervice, and well known to, and intimate

mate with, Mr. Hankey's brother, or he would not have taken such a liberty.

As appearances were for him, Mr. Hankey said, that his brother would be in town that day, and would dine with him at five o'clock, at which time Mr. Semple was desired to call, and actually invited to dinner. To a man of less *nonchalance* than James George Semple, this answer would have been a complete rebuff. But his motto was, " *In for a penny, in for a pound.*" He thanked Mr. Hankey, and boldly accepted the invitation.

At a quarter before five, having called in his out-posts of humour, anecdote, tale, and repartee, and joined them with his main guard, *Impudence,* he knocked at Mr. Hankey's door.—The servants ushered him up stairs, and he was introduced to the Mr. Hankeys. The brother, whom Mr. Semple pretended to be so intimate with, professed he had not the smallest knowledge of him; when our Hero reminded him of this, that, and the other Gentleman, with whom Mr. Hankey had been at such and such places; assured him, that he, Mr. Semple, was often of the party, and lamented much the want of Mr. Hankey's recollection. The servant having announced dinner, they all sat down, and the Major began to file off his out-posts. As his conversation was entertaining, they were in no great hurry to lose their visitor; but when the subject of the visit came on the carpet, as men of business they declined the request.

So far unfortunate, Mr. Semple set his wits to work. A smaller sum, he said, perhaps would do to extricate his friend; and if Mr. Hankey would

would advance him five guineas, on a security of five guineas per annum on the Compassionate List at the Pay-Office, he was ready to give Mr. Hankey a draught on Mr. Thomas, at the Office, who paid the money.

It being a case of some seeming compassion, interwoven with a delicacy in refusing a Gentleman whom they had invited to dinner, Mr. Hankey advanced him the money, and Semple wrote the following letter.

S I R,

Mr. Hankey, of Fenchurch-street, has been kind enough to advance me five guineas on my promise of giving no other order to receive the small pension on the Compassionate List but to him. I declare upon my honour that this is the only obligation I either have or shall give, and that when due to him and no other person—I will send the certificate.

I am, Sir,

London, *July* 4, 1786.

With much consideration,

Your most obedient servant,

J. G. Semple.

Directed to

Mr. Thomas,

Pay-Office,

Whitehall,

London.

F   Now

Now the truth is, he was not, nor ever was, on the Compaſſionate Liſt.—In faƈt, Mrs. Semple was.—Nor could he even receive the money for her, unleſs ſhe was preſent; for, it being payable to Mrs. Semple, even her certificate, order, or power of attorney, would be no juſtification of the payment; ſhe muſt receive it in perſon; and as Mr. Thomas knows and performs his duty with as much exaƈtneſs as fidelity, he certainly never would pay Mr. Hankey on any ſuch certificate of Mr. Semple's. We are afraid, therefore, that the conſciouſneſs of having done, what Mr. Hankey conceived, a generous aƈt, muſt be his ſole reward.

By contraſting this conduƈt with the following little ſpecimen of his abilities, the Reader muſt ſoon ſee the different degrees of light and ſhade in his compoſition. This ſame James George Semple, who could introduce himſelf to Baron Hompeſch and Meſſrs. Hankeys, had been running about the town all day in an hackney-coach, and by ſtepping into Mr. Francis Sykes's, in South-Audley-ſquare, under a pretended buſineſs, he bilked the poor fellow of his whole fare.

In ſhort, the noblemen's houſes he frequented daily under this device, made his perſon as familiar to the great as to the little world. The title of Major became as alarming as the appearance of a wolf at Spa during the winter ſeaſon, and the doors became equally guarded againſt his entering them. The compariſon holds good, with this degree of difference; the wolf prouls at midnight, Major Semple ravaged at noon-day.

By

By this practice of his, the reader muſt obſerve that no character or reputation was ſafe when a guinea was the object of Mr. Semple.

Should any perſon be ſurpriſed at his ſucceſs, we beg him to recollect an anecdote of the late celebrated Dr. Rock.

He was ſtanding one day at his door on Ludgate-hill, when a real doctor of phyſic paſſed, who had learning and abilities, but whoſe modeſty was the true cauſe of his poverty: "How comes it," ſays he to the quack, "that you, without educa-
"tion, without ſkill, without the leaſt knowledge
"of the ſcience, are enabled to live in the ſtyle
"you do?—You keep your town-houſe, your
"carriage, and your country-houſe; whilſt I,
"allowed to poſſeſs ſome knowledge, have nei-
"ther, and can hardly pick up a ſubſiſtence!—
"Why, look ye," ſaid Rock, ſmiling, "how
"many people do you think have paſſed ſince you
"aſked me the queſtion?"—"Why," anſwered the doctor, "perhaps a hundred."—"And how
"many out of that hundred, think you, poſſeſs
"common ſenſe?"—"Poſſibly one," anſwered the doctor. "Then," ſaid Rock, "that one
"comes to you; and I take care to get the other
"ninety-nine!"

In conformity to that doctrine, Mr. Semple met a repulſe in Mr. Clark, ſadler, of Great Portland-ſtreet. He attempted to obtain two ſaddles by the name of Major Gray, an American officer; but Mr. Clark, being the one out of the foregoing hundred, declined the trouble of executing the order.

Mr.

Mr. Cecil, shoe-maker, of Leadenhall-street, was not, however, quite so much on his guard as Mr. Clark. He came to that gentleman in the name of Major Harrold, and ordered two pair of boots and some shoes to be sent to him, by a stage-coach, down to Park Hall, whither he was immediately going. The order was completed, and sent. Two days after, Mr. Cecil's journey-man espied Major Harrold at the Queen's Arms, Newgate-street. The Major was confused, nay he even blushed. He desired the man to make his compliments to his master, and tell him that he would call and payhim in a day or two, and begged that the man would not mention his seeing him to any body else, as he was in town on very particular and private business,

At Messieurs Dixon and Co. of Aldgate, shoe-makers, he played the same game as he had done with Mr. Cecil; but with these gentlemen he found the name of Semple inconvenient, and therefore assumed that of Major Kennedy.

In the name of Major Grant (pretending that he came from Petersburgh on an embassy to this court, and that he had business with Mr. Pitt) he had the same success with Mr. Stewart, per-fumer, Broad-street; and obtained articles of per-fumery to a degree that enabled him to completely stock the toilette of a fine gentleman ; for which the Major now stands indicted. And to sweeten his tooth, as well as his person, he applied to Mr. Andrews, of Wimpole-street, fruiterer, and was no less successful in the name of Major Stewart.

Innkeepers

Innkeepers alfo, as well as keepers of hotels and coffee-houfes, experienced his ufual diligence. Of Mr. Bolton of the Saracen's-Head, Aldgate, he borrowed two guineas in the name of J. G. Harrold, Efquire; which when he borrowed under the pretence of wanting cafh to difcharge fome hackney-coach hire and charges for the carriage of goods, he wrote the above name in Mr. Bolton's book. On receiving the cafh, the Major took the pen and defaced it, faying it was too trifling a fum for *his* name to remain in a book about. It however remains clear to be feen; and it is equally clear, that, trifling as the fum was, it ftill remains unpaid.

We have already ftated that he obtained a carriage of Mr. Lycett, of White-Chapel, coach-maker. But as a horfe to ride is of no ufe without a faddle, fo a carriage is of no ufe without horfes to draw it. For this purpofe he applied to Mr. Tatterfall, of Hyde-Park Corner, and purchafed two horfes, for which he gave a draught on Drummonds. The value of that draught the reader may readily guefs. It was not worth the five guineas Mr. Tatterfall lent him; for Major Semple had not at that time any loofe cafh about him, and he had alfo once more unfortunately left his purfe on the table. The great convenience of thefe horfes was to draw away Mr. Lycett's carriage; and for a few days Major Semple lived in as fplendid a ftyle as if he had been on full pay.

Nor did Mr. Fozard, ftable-keeper, of Park-Lane, efcape the Major's obfervation. Under pretence of extenfive acquaintances and high connections, he obtained fome credit, and borrowed a folia solitary guinea, which he was reduced to, he said, by losing his purse by an accidental fall from his horse. But Mr. Fozard having taken some little pains to satisfy himself about the Major, they were the means of producing the following letter from him.

I am Cursedly persecuted for the few things that I owe, which all together, even including yours, don't make forty pounds, the money I have spent since I have been in Town prevents me from having it in my power to Apply for any more. There is yet a good sum due me, which I shall certainly receive before the end of the week or thereabouts, and even this day if I durst come up to Town I was to have had paid me a small sum which is sufficient to clear me of your debt. I came yesterday down here where I mean to remain till I have satisfied the demands that are against me, an acquaintance who comes to London this day will deliver you this, he I hope will also receive the money for me, I expected. I beg it of you to be assured that I will pay you, the time is now drawing near on which I promised to pay every thing, sure no man was ever so much talked of or teazed for so trifling a debt as mine are, there has been more pains took to hurt me, than ever there was any man. I can prove having spent and paid above 300l. in the first 2 or 3 weeks of my arrivall in London and what I owe as I told you before wont make 40l. the noise they have made has prevented them from being paid for they hurted my credit so much, that I am afraid to ask any body to assist me, I could easily have borrowed more money than would have cleared me if they had let me alone Mr. Dalby certainly was very kind to me at first but he talked a great deal afterward; however the assistance he gave me I shall
never

never forget and moft undoubtedly will pay him. I think I can truft to your not taking there example and you may be affured that I will pay you

I am Sir

Monday Morning 8 oClock
Woolwich.

Your moft Obedient
Servant
J. G. SEMPLE.

PRAY, DON'T MENTION WHERE I AM.

Directed to Mr. Fozard.

The reader need not be reminded that this letter was not written at Woolwich, for the Major was then in the Spring-Garden coffee-houfe.

In one of his exploits, however, there feems to have been a momentary impulfe of generous honefty. He had been rattling about the town, as ufual, in an hackney-coach, and had, as ufual, bilked the coachman, by leaving him and the coach in waiting in Windmill-ftreet, near the Haymarket. He called at Mr. Skillern's muſic-fhop, in St. Martin's Lane, the corner of St. Martin's church-yard, and begged Mr. Skillern would fend up his man to tell the coachman not to wait, but to call the next day at Mr. Skillern's at two o'clock, and the money fhould be left for him. Mr. Skillern, although a ftranger to the Major, (nor could he recollect him, notwithstanding the latter wanted to perfuade him he had been a great cuftomer) fent his man up, during which time Major Semple explained the reafon by faying, He was purfued by bailiffs, and could not return to the coach. The coachman certainly called; but the above feeming momentary impulfe of generous honefty never again influenced the breaft of the Major.

A fimilar

A fimilar inftance of his ingenuity he had practifed on another coachman, who was more fortunate than his preceding brother-whip. He happened afterwards to meet Major Semple as he was
driving his hackney-coach up Bedford-Row, in
company with another gentleman, who, on the
coachman's jumping off the box, thought proper
to decamp. Having brufhed up to the Major,
and being determined not to quit him, the latter went to feveral houfes in the neighbourhood
to borrow the fum of 1*l*. 13*s*. but was fo unfortunate as not to fucceed. His wits, however, being pufhed hard, he bethought himfelf of Mrs.
Watfon, a lady who lives in Gloucefter-ftreet,
No. 42 : thither he and the coachman went. He
recollected that Lord Verney had lodged there.
To this lady he applied, under the fanction of being his Lordfhip's friend, and having vifited him
there, for the above fum to difcharge the demand :
he promifed the coachman at firft to call the next
day at Mrs. Watfon's to leave the money; but
this promife not being deemed fatisfactory, and
offering to go, the coachman refolutely (how
legally is another thing) locked Mrs. Watfon's
door upon, and fwore the Major fhould not march
without he was paid. Mrs. Watfon, feeing the
gentleman thus diftreffed, promifed to pay it the
next day if the Major did not. The coachman
was fatisfied, and departed; as did the Major,
with every promife and every apology he could
fuggeft. Apologies and promifes coft him nothing. He never returned; and Mrs. Watfon was
fummoned by the coachman to the court of re-
quefts; and, rather than appear at fuch a repu-
table

table and critical appendage to law and juftice, fhe paid the debt.

Hitherto we have treated our readers with a few of his ingenious devices in the metropolis. His abilities, however, were not fo circumfcribed as to be confined to one fcene of action. The country experienced his exploits in a manner no lefs diffufive than in town. The two following we felect.

Having been obliged to a recefs from a very laborious feafon of public bufinefs, he took an excurfion Northward. At Leicefter he put up at the fign of the Three Crowns, kept by Mr. Bifhop. Under the ftale pretence of having left his pocket-book in town, he was, he faid, unfortunately without cafh to purfue his journey to Derby. Mr. Bifhop, taking Mr. Semple for what he really was not, viz. a gentleman, generoufly accommodated the unfortunate traveller with five guineas, in order to enable him to purfue his journey to Derby, for which Major Semple as freely gave Mr. Bifhop the following valuable fecurity.

Leicefter, Aug. 15th, 1785.

£. 5 : 5 : 0

   At fight pleafe to pay to Meffrs. Coart and Swayne, or Order, the fum of Five Guineas, which you will place to my account.

         Wm. Bishop.

  Accepd J. G. Semple

  To J. G. Semple Efquire
Spring Garden Coffee Houfe,
  London.

    C   Had

Had the above acceptance been duly honoured, we never fhould have had the opportunity of taking a copy of it. We fhall therefore difmifs this piece of ingenuity with obferving, that the Major's expences at Mr. Bifhop's (for he lived in fome ftyle) arofe to as much as the draught, both which were fatisfied much in the fame way.

But, having travelled with the Major to Leicefter, we beg the reader will march with us a little farther; and at Matlock in Derbyfhire we will indulge ourfelves with a halt.

At Matlock Mr. Semple found it convenient to ftay a few days, during which time he ingratiated himfelf into the company of feveral gentlemen; two of whom he knew, and on whom the Major exerted the utmoft efforts of his avocations.

He foon fcraped an acquaintance with a Mr. T——, a gentleman who lives in town; and having found out, as Scrub fays, who he was, where he came from, and whither he was going, the Major opened his battery. He talked of his great fervices to government, his intimacy with the gentleman who is now the Chancellor of the Exchequer, Mr. Pitt; produced a letter of that gentleman's to him; and, in fhort, conveyed into the mind of Mr. T. fo high an opinion of his rank and confequence, that on his requeft Mr. T. readily accommodated him with ten guineas: but what the pretence was by which he obtained it we have forgot.

We have given the reader a fhort bait at Matlock, and now beg leave to conduct him back to Leicefter, where the Major declined troubling Mr. Bifhop. Perhaps he thought that a free horfe

ought

ought not to be rode to death; and therefore he put up at Mr. Allamand's, the Three Cranes, where Mr. Semple appeared as great a gentleman as he had done at Mr. Bishop's, and where Mr. Allamand treated him with equal civility.

From Leicester the Major came to town; and as during his stay at Matlock he had been industrious in cultivating those acquaintances which were most likely to add to his respect and interest, so on his arrival here he was equally active in improving those two material circumstances in life.

Mr. R. a respectable bookseller of New Bond-street, under the recommendation and acquaintance which Major Semple assumed with a gentleman, (whom he had honoured with his company in Germany, and thereby discovered that he dealt with Mr. R.) lent him several guineas at different times for an equal number of ducats, which said ducats the Major left in pledge with Mr. R. but quite forgot ever to redeem.

Under a similar pretence he visited Mr. Jameson, bookseller, of the Strand, in the name of Major Cunningham; and left behind him, recorded in black and white, a fact that reflects equal honour on his dexterity.

At Mr. Banfield's, woollen-draper, No. 444, Strand, the Major also gave proofs of his singular abilities, by gaining credit for cloth for liveries, &c. &c. And Mr. Chowles, hatter, in Duke-street, Portland-street, behind Portland Chapel, on the 5th of July last, was kind enough to leave a hat at the bar of George's Coffee-house, for the Major's use, directed for J. Wilson, Esq. to

which

which was added—Pay nineteen shillings. When
the Major's hand was in, he might have written
nineteen pounds: it would have made no difference to Mr. Chowles. But, as

‘ There is a tide, in the affairs of men,
‘ Which, taken at the flood, leads on to FORTUNE;’

so James George Semple, Esq. panting after the
favours of so fickle a goddess, nobly plunged
himself at last into the full tide, which safely conducted him into port; *id est*, his Majesty's jail of
Newgate, from whence that said FORTUNE has so
often dangled many a great man into eternity,
with all the honours due to the important services
which he had so bravely lavished on his king and
country. In plain English, the Major visited
Mr. Feltham, hatter, in Fleet-street, in February
last; and in the following manner, as it appeared
before the Lord Mayor, conferred the same favour
on that gentleman he had so liberally bestowed
on many others. He called at Mr. Feltham's,
in a chariot, attended by two footmen; and,
after informing him of his having been recommended by Mr. Richardson, who he understood was his particular friend, he then produced a lady's riding-hat as a pattern for Mr. F.
at the same time ordering him to make two of
the same kind with all possible expedition, as he
intended to take them to Russia, and at that
time told Mr. F. that he was a Major in the
Russian army.

Mr. F——, perceiving that the pattern which
the Major had was made by him, agreeable to
directions from Mr. Richardson, for Baron Hompesch,

pefch, a fhort time before, was fatisfied that every thing the fuppofed Major had uttered was founded in truth. The Major, after giving his directions to Mr. F——, went away, returned the next day in a hackney-coach, and at going requefted his man to call another coach. Mr. F——, at this, expreffed his furprife at his changing coaches, obferving to him, that, in confequence of the late regulation for hackney-coaches, it muft become very expenfive. The other faid, he felt it rather an *uneafy* one, and had a glafs in the back, which was difagreeable to him. Another coach was then called, and the prifoner departed. That the next day he called again, urged the finifhing of the two ladies hats, paid Mr. F—— fome compliments on his fuperior ftyle of cocking, and befpoke one for his own wear: he then told Mr. F. that he had a bill on a merchant in the city for a hundred pounds, and that he would then go and receive it. Mr. F. afked to fee the bill, as in all probability he could direct him to the houfe, which would fave the trouble of enquiring elfe-where: this he however declined, and departed. The next day he called again, faid he had juft arrived in his brother's carriage from the country; but that being drove at an immoderate rate up to town, and being obliged to return to dinner, would be under the neceffity of hiring poft-horfes, as he could not think of harraffing his brother's; and requefted Mr. F. to lend him three guineas in gold, and half a guinea in filver, for the convenience of paying the turnpikes. Mr. F. having light gold in his pockets, and apprehen-five of its caufing difappointment to the Major,

borrowed

borrowed three new guineas from his next-door neighbour; which, with half a guinea in filver, he gave to the prifoner. On the Major's quitting the fhop, a perfon at the door afked Mr. F. if he knew him; and, on anfwering in the affirmative, was told by the ftranger that he was miftaken; that he was Semple, the notorious fharper; but refufed Mr. F. the power of making ufe of his name, which prevented Mr. F. from purfuing him at that time. Being however fomewhat alarmed, he went to his friend Mr. Richardfon, who he imagined had recommended him; that Mr. Richardfon denied ever having done fo, and declared he would not truft him for a guinea, as he attempted to take him in for 40l. He then referred Mr. F. to Mr. G. of the Temple, who confirmed Mr. R.'s account of the prifoner, and recounted many other fraudulent acts of which he had been guilty. That from that time (Feb. 22) Mr. F. confidered himfelf bound, by an indifpenfable obligation, to bring to public juftice a man who could, without remorfe, make a profeffion of diftreffing the unwary; and that from that time he had taken every poffible means of apprehending the prifoner, which, by his fteady perfeverance, had, at length proved effectual. That, in the courfe of his inquiries after the Major, he had been able to trace out fome of the moft nefarious acts that ever difgraced an individual. Having fome time ago received intelligence of his haunts, he procured a warrant; and, after being repeatedly difappointed in apprehending him, as he was paffing through Cheapfide, perceiving a coach anfwering the defcription of that

ufed

ufed by Semple, he inftantly called to the driver to ftop, but without effect: he then purfued the carriage, and after a long chace attempted to leap in at the window; upon which the coachman ftopped, and the Major efcaped out of the oppofite fide. Mr. F. purfued. The Major then took fhelter in a banker's fhop, where he remained till the arrival of the officers from Bow-ftreet, who conducted him in fafety to Mr. Addington, who tranfmitted him to the Lord Mayor of London for examination.

So eminent a gentleman being committed to prifon, he foon became the topic of every company; and the public prints were equally as induftrious to propagate his fame, as the world at large had been. We have felected the following, as it leads to a very curious reply of Mr. Semple's.

MORNING POST.

Mr. Feltham, who has fpiritedly ftepped forward to curb the induftrious hero Major Semple in his career, affigned to the Lord Mayor, as reafons for a fecond examination, that feveral other charges of the fame nature, more forcible than his, could be produced. Above 120 perfons attended, who propofed to prove a multitude of fimilar facts againft the prifoner; but the Lord Mayor decided againft the neceffity of their appearance, as the cafe of Mr. F. was fufficiently ftrong in itfelf to fupport a profecution, and enfure the penalties of the law to the offender. His Lordfhip expreffed his thanks to Mr. F. for the fpirit he fhewed in following up the delinquent. The groupe who fuffered by the artifices of this genius, recited

many

many and various exploits which peculiarly dif-
tinguished his ingenuity. Among several, he
contrived to swindle to a town in Derbyshire, by
taking in one side of the road on his departure,
and the other on his return; in which he succeeded. He at another time assumed the character of an ambassador to the court of Russia,
and nearly ruined an unfortunate taylor, who
prepared for him a wardrobe to near the value of
400l. a considerable part of which was delivered.
He travelled to Russia, whence the effects of his
genius forced him to make a precipitate retreat
to Sweden; from the capital of which his quarters
were also beat up. In Flanders he succeeded
upon the credulity of the public; and Calais did
not escape the effects of his industry.

He is married into a family who are far from
deserving the consequences of such a connection.
He has a wife whose character is irreproachable,
by whom he had two children: he abandoned
her, and took up with an unhappy woman, whom
he has brought to ruin.

The Answer.

To the Printer of the Morning Chronicle.

" Sir,

" I am too sensible of the difficulty of vindica-
ting my character to make the attempt; yet I would
willingly shew to the public, through the channel
of your unbiassed paper, that I am grossly injured,
and

and that nothing can authorize the assertions which have appeared in the public prints, but the unhappy situation into which my follies (to give them no severer a name) have thrown me. Mr. Feltham, as yet the only person bound over to prosecute, has not hesitated to do his utmost to hurt me. He occasioned my appearing a second time at Guildhall, under the pretence of having twenty-three people to appear against me; but on calling over their names, two only were to be found. The whole of Mr. Feltham's conduct towards me has been marked; during the examination of Mr. D. shoemaker, (who could not make any story out) he went so far as to call to him in the presence of the whole court, "Don't you remember what you said to me this "morning?" I remarked that circumstance immediately to the Lord Mayor; and, I believe, it had a proper effect.

"The papers have been filled with many different charges against me : the impossibility of answering them must be visible to every body; I reserve them for another occasion. Sometime ago a story, without any ground whatever, was fabricated, about my personating a certain noble Marquis, and swindling two maiden sisters out of their whole fortune, 1500l. This story, groundless as it was, and contradicted with authority, has again been repeated. It is also asserted, that I have nearly

H ruined

ruined a taylor, by assuming the character of an am-
baffador to the court of Ruffia, and obtaining from
him cloaths to the amount of 400l. May I beg to
know the name of this taylor? and if the perfon
who gave the intelligence is not, from motives of
fear or fhame, obliged to conceal his, I fhould be
glad to be indulged with it. It is alfo faid, that I
was obliged to make a precipitate retreat from the
capital of Sweden: in anfwer to this, I can only
fay, that I have been in almoft every capital in
Europe; the capital of Sweden I never was in during my life, and, as I have faid before, it is almoft
the only one.

"I cannot fuppofe any other reafon for filling
the papers with thefe groundlefs charges againft
me, but the malicious intention of injuring me in
the eyes of thofe who have fome friendfhip for me,
and the ftill more wicked one of prejudicing the
judges and jury againft me. I am forry to confefs,
there are people who may with reafon complain of
me; Mr. Feltham certainly with truth cannot. I
declare I will do my endeavours to fettle as foon as
poffible all the demands againft me.

"I ought not to finifh this without taking particular notice of the very humane treatment I have
received from the Lord Mayor: the kind attentions
of Mr. Miller, the city marfhal, merit my warm-
eft acknowledgments. Since my confinement I
have

have received every indulgence that the keeper of the prifon can with propriety give me.

I am, Sir;

Your moft obedient,

And very humble fervant;

July, 18, 1786.   J. G. SEMPLE."

To comment upon this would be making a parade, and a wafte of pen, ink, and paper. It was our duty to give it becaufe the *audi alteram partem* ought never to be departed from. One obfervation only we beg leave to make : the Major acknowledges having been in almoft every court in Europe but that of Sweden, and that court he denies ever having been in. Mark the pofition, and then what, from his own affertion, is the natural conclufion ? Why, that the *precipitate retreat* was not from Sweden, but from fome other court in Europe, moft of which he allows he has been at. When great men commit blunders, they are fure to be monftrous ones. Had Major, or James George Semple, Efq. or Mr. Semple, made no anfwer, it would have afforded no room to litigate his literary abilities. Had Peterfburg been fubftituted for Copenhagen, the Major muft have been mute.

But being now in *falva cuftodia*, and the Major left to his private meditations, we muft beg the reader to drop him till the period of his appearance at the bar of the Old Bailey, which was on Tuef-

H 2   day

day the 24th of July laft; where he made his entré, with the Turnkey of Newgate on one fide, and a certain knight of the poft, vulgarly called Jack Ketch, on the other, to anfwer a charge made by Mr. Lycett; vide page 46.

The Major bowed to the court—he bowed to the jury—he bowed to the audience—three bows. —His honourable attendants, by the power of fenfitive fympathy, bowed alfo—They felt the force of attraction in—the neck. Whilft they bowed, a fide-glance of commiferation darted on the Major, who blufhed full as much as a modern made peer when introduced by two of his friends, at the bar of a ftill greater affembly, with all his bluſhing honours about him.

He marched majeftically forward—He was called on to—hold up his hand! Degrading humiliation! Nothing moves one fo much as a great man in diftrefs! He was infulted with all the infolence of official interrogation, and afked, "How "fay you, James George Harrold, otherwiſe "Semple, otherwiſe Kennedy; are you GUILTY "of this FELONY of which you ftand indicted, or not "GUILTY?" Any anfwer to fuch a queftion, put to fuch a gentleman, would have been a derogation of character: nay, fo truly pitiable was his fituation, that it——moved the court; for, as Ariftophanes fays, in his Devil upon Two Sticks—" Up ftarted "little Belzy in the form of an able practitioner," and faid—

He

He humbly conceived that his client could not anfwer the queftion; and by a delicate turn relieved the Major from the moft poignant diftrefs. This *delicate turn* was, A FLAW in the Indictment. This he prefaced with an obfervation, That it was his own wifh, it was the wifh of his client, to meet the indictment upon the merits; and not to avail themfelves of any legal inaccuracies. But from the complexion of this profecution, or rather perfecution, he thought it his duty to lay hold of every opportunity which could operate to Mr. Semple's advantage, (his counfel in this introductory addrefs dropt the title of Major) and therefore he took an exception to the indictment. This objection, he faid, was founded upon ftat. 1. Hen. 5th, c. 5, which enacts, that in all Indictments, the party indicted fhould be defcribed in the Indictment, with proper additions; and he cited Hales P. Crown, B. ii. ch. 25, fec. 70.

He alfo argued, that this being an indictment for felony, it is a fatal fault to apply the addition to the name which comes under the *alias dictus* only, and not to the firft name, though it is not material whether any addition be put to the name which comes under the *alias dictus* or not, becaufe what is fo expreffed is not material; but it is fo great an error to omit an addition to his firft name, that where feveral are indicted, fuch an omiffion, in refpect to one of them, vitiates the Indictment

as

as to all: 1 Bulstrode 183, 2 Leonard 183, Cro. Eliz. 583, Dyer 88.

He relied strongly on Hooper's case, 2 Leon. 183; and cited several other authorities.

The judge, Mr. Recorder, observed, that the modern practice was uniformly contrary to the cases cited, but allowed the legality of the objection.

His counsel contended, that allowing the practice to be so, the Court ought to over-rule it, on its being shewn to be contrary to law.

Mr. Recorder admitted the practice to be against the objection; but thought the proper mode of objection would have been by plea in abatement or demurrer.

His counsel again contended, that where there was a wrong addition, the proper mode of taking advantage of it was by plea in abatement, where there was no addition, or the objection appeared upon the face of the Indictment, and in the present case, the addition being to the *alias dictus* only, therefore no addition, the proper mode of objecting was by exception.

He further contended, that if a word of substance be omitted in the Indictment, the whole Indictment is bad; but it is otherwise where a word of form is omitted, or there is an omission of an anonymous word when the sense is the same. 2 Hawk. 246.

The

The King *v.* Wheelhoufe, *Popham* 208. An Indictment for frequenting a bawdy-houfe, and Serjeant Crawley moved to quafh it as infufficient; and among many other objections faid, the Indictment ftated that the defendant was *noctivagus,* and it did not fay that he was a fufpicious night-walker. But Dodridge and Whitlock J. over-ruled this objection, and the defendant received judgment. Hilary, 2 Car. King's Bench; and it was determined in Willow's cafe, *Latch* 173.

Under all thefe confiderations he moved the court to quafh the indictment.

The Recorder thought the objection was well-founded, and ordered that the indictment fhould be quafhed accordingly.

In plain Englifh, and to make this recital intelligible to men of common fenfe, as well as to lawyers, let it be underftood, that the prifoner, (we beg the Major's pardon) was indicted thus:

The jurors for our Lord the King, on their oath prefent, That JAMES GEORGE HARROLD, *otherwife* SEMPLE, *otherwife* KENNEDY, &c. &c. &c. whereas in truth and in fact it ought to have ran thus:

The jurors for our Lord the King, on their oath prefent, That JAMES GEORGE SEMPLE, *otherwife* HARROLD, *otherwife* KENNEDY, &c. &c. &c. becaufe his real name being SEMPLE, that name ought to have *taken the lead,* and the Alias's, like fo many other horfes

horfes that have ftarted for the *King's plate*, been
whipped in for the fweepftakes only.

But his counfel having been fuccefsful in this
motion, made another, which unfortunately failed.
The indictment having, by order of court, been
quafhed, he moved that Mr. Semple be DISCHARG-
ID. The Recorder, however, demurred to this
motion, by faying, That on difcuffing the *form*
of an indictment, the court never go into the *me-*
rits; that as a grand jury had thought proper to fay
the prifoner had been guilty of felony, it would be a
breach of duty in the court to fuffer him to go at
large till that queftion was tried.

He therefore ordered Major Semple to be taken
thence to the place from whence he came, and to
be detained in his Majefty jail of Newgate till the
next feffions, when the profecutor might have an
opportunity of preferring a frefh bill, and then alter
the form of the indictment.

It was *hinted* befides, that there were feveral
other indictments againft him for *frauds*, which
were of themfelves ftrong enough to detain him.

The counfel then obferved that he fhould advife
his client to plead and take his trial; but after
fome confideration, that intention was dropped, and
the Major taken from the bar, bowing three times
as he retired.

We ought here to obferve, that we cannot poffibly mean any the moft diftant reflection on the gentleman

tleman who was Major Semple's counsel, Mr. Agar, by adopting the term " *Little Belzy.*" It would hurt us, not a little, should he so conceive it. We know his liberality of sentiment, and that he will readily pardon a little of the Old Bailey wit. Indeed, to do him justice, he distinguished himself much to his credit, and with a modesty that discovered as much the characteristics of a gentleman, as with a learning that displayed his abilities as a lawyer. We know his manners in private life to be amiable; and we have no doubt, by application, he will very soon be an equal ornament to his profession as he is already to society.

Disappointed, therefore, in concluding the life of Major Semple with his trial *now*; the recess has afforded us an opportunity of making the delay agreeable, by treating our readers in the mean time with a few more anecdotes.

From the circumstance of Baron Hompesch having introduced him to Mr. Chancellor Pitt, Mr. Semple struck out a line of ingenuity which seldom or never failed of success. He took the freedom, as one gentleman might readily do with another, of writing to Mr. Pitt; and in one of these letters hinted a scheme which, he said, would be serviceable to the kingdom, desiring to know when Mr. Pitt would do him the honour of an audience.

Having obtained answers, which was all that Mr. Semple thought necessary for the good of his country, he took that natural advantage of it,

I   which

which lefs ambitious minds might be excufed for. He boafted of his acquaintance and intimacy with Mr. Pitt, readily fhewed his letters, and alfo letters from Dr. Prettyman, and made himfelf of that confequence which he knew the weaker part of the world readily bowed down to.

The firft inftance we have on record of his making ufe of his correfpondence, is on the 19th of December, in the year 1785, at Doncafter in Yorkfhire.—We have not learnt the particulars how he got there, whether it was in a journey to Scotland or from it; nor how he introduced himfelf to the gentleman who gave credit to that correfpondence: but the façt is, he did introduce himfelf, and the introduçtion anfwered his then purpofe. The ingenious tale too, which he fabricated to complete his purpofe, we are alfo ftrangers to; but the following letter, which a very fortunate accident put into our poffeffion, exhibits fo very pleafing and humorous a piçture, and is alfo accompanied with fuch a farcaftic turn, that we infert it *litera fcriptis*, as the beft explanation of our gentleman's addrefs.

SIR   *Doncafter July 20th 1786*
        Yorkfhire

IT was my intention in April laft to have done myfelf the Honor of paying my refpeçts to you or to have attempted it at W B Blands Efq' N° 24 queen Anns ftreet Weft London—But truly as you fay by your ad-
             drefs

dreſs to the publick in the Morning Chronicle of 17ᵗʰ
dated 15 *inſtant*

Various Acctˢ then circulating—made me defer adding
trouble to my ſo readily being duped by you the 19ᵗʰ Decʳ
1785—For 7¼ Guineas

" *You confeſs there are people who may with reaſon complain, of you*, And do add " *I declare I will do my endeavor
to ſettle as ſoon as poſſible all the demands againſt me.*" Wou'd
it was known to this Houſe *Elliſon Cooke & Co* when to
expect it. Can you remember all that paſs'd—And where
the James Semple poiſoned himſelf! who I mention'd to
you had Swindled me in 1777—Its a long time ſince—
Forgive me if I trouble you with ſome more particulars of
this Laſt matter *James Semple* (ſo like your writing I've
no doubt the very ſame perſon as wrote J G Semple)
" York 24 Octr 1777 pay *Mr Thoˢ Swan* 5 Gˢ addreſs'd
to Mr. Veach Merᵗ Broad Street Golden Square London."
When this made its way to Town the Accᵗ was Mr
Swann was Swindled—Don't you think ſuch Villains de-
ſerve Hanging Mr Semple? May all ſuch only meet their
deſerts—And *ſome Folks* might not have had the trouble to
live ſo long—as ever to experience any diſagreeable trial
to pay debts—ſo long diſhonorably contracted—Judge
you by the encloſ'd—And at leaſt if not for both or *all
three Se i* mples! not forgetting your very ſerious promiſe
Words in decr Laſt do ſomething worthy yourſelf and my
advertiſing you in the Morning Chronicle, or any paper
you chuſe——That you have diſcharged the 5 & 7 Guineas
& ¼ at our Bankers Meſſrˢ R & F Goſling you may remember you took their names down in december Laſt—
You may depend upon my doing every generous act towards you in return—But as I greatly fear the pleaſing
ſide—for myſelf—Will not do that to myſelf—I truly wiſh
every VILLAIN had adminiſter'd to him—Twelve Guineas

I 2

&

& ⅓ payment wou'd be more agreeable to receive than to
join in the profecuting the once fo Intimate Friend of our
GREAT Mr Pit & his fecretary Mr Smith——But wch
I fhall have a pleafure in doing—If your Friends want
help who have got you into fuch obligations as you exprefs
to the Lord Mayor and City Marfhall.

My name already you have herein.

It appears, by the foregoing letter, that a Mr.
Semple had paid his refpects to the gentleman nine
years ago; and, by the prefent Mr. Semple's account, had poifoned himfelf. What the gentleman's
opinion was of the two Sofia's may be eafily guelfed
by his interrogation, *Don't you think fuch villains de-
ferve hanging, Mr. Semple?*

It muft be alfo obferved, that although the gentleman gave himfelf the trouble of addrelfing Mr.
Semple on the fubject, which is eafily feen was
fince his unlucky confinement, fuch addrefs was
not the refult of any the moft diftant idea of being refunded the foregoing fum, but from the pleafing fatisfaction of reminding Mr. Semple that the
matter was not totally forgot, and that he was not
entirely a ftranger to his prefent place of abode.

Indeed, the gentleman's good wifhes towards
Mr. Semple are by no means fo favourable as his
calamitous circumftances may require, as he promifes him, if his friends want help, he fhall have a
pleafure in affifting them.

We have hitherto traced Mr. Semple's abilities

in

in preying upon the purfes of his friends; but
that qualification was infinitely inferior to his
merit in preying upon the peace of mind and
happinefs of two gentlemen, who had the honour
of his acquaintance.

It has been noticed already that he made his
application to Baron Hompefch on the ground of
having fought two duels himfelf, and killed both
his men; but he was more fortunate in the following event.

When he was at Spa, there happened to be a
quarrel between two real gentlemen, with whom
Mr. Semple affociated, and he was the go-between
in the difpute. To each party, though he under-
took the office of a mediator, he aggravated the
expreffions of the one, and thereby inflamed the
mind of the other. This diverfion of Mr. Semple's produced a duel; and the confequence was,
that one of his friends was wounded : but when a
reconciliation and explanation enfued, Mr. Semple thought proper, in order to avoid manual chaf-
tifement, to abdicate the place.

Mr. Semple was alfo in November 1785, at Manchefter, and had introduced himfelf to feveral gentlemen as the confidential and bofom friend of Mr.
Pitt, Dr. Prettyman, Mr. Rofe, Mr. Lepine, and
others who have the management of the various de-
partments of his Majefty's treafury. By producing
of fome letters, which he had artfully obtained from
fome

some of those gentlemen, he had made himself a man of no small consequence in that country. But his application to Thomas Butterworth Bayley, Esq. of the Hope, near Manchester, who is in the commission of the peace for that county, likewise a gentleman of independent fortune, and, what is still far superior, a most respectable character, was founded on another claim.

Mr. Semple introduced himself to that gentleman as a relation of the noble family of Lord Semple, of Scotland, with whom he knew Mr. Bayley and his father had been acquainted, and even connected; and, to induce him to believe he was the person he represented himself, he exhibited treasury letters from different persons in that department; his plea of wanting money was, that having been a long journey on a matrimonial excursion with a young lady of great fortune from the west of England to Dover, and from thence to Gretna-Green, in Scotland, his cash was expended. The sum Mr. Bayley lent him was fifteen guineas (not twenty-five pounds, as related in the former editions) for which he gave excellent security, his note. Mr. Bayley considering this as a fraud, wrote to Sir Sampson Wright on the subject, who was very active in his endeavours to have him apprehended.

We

We hardly need fay, that the note was never re-deemed; but when Mr. Semple had the honour of being conducted to the domicil of our fovereign lord the king, and to cut fo confpicuous a figure in our public prints, Mr. Bayley by that means difcovering the Major's abode, indorfed the note over to Sir Sampfon, who has been fo unkind as to lodge a detainer againft Mr. Semple in the fhape and form of an uncivil action.

Now, though the foregoing fum of money, thus borrowed of Mr. Bayley, was obtained in a manner that moft affuredly comes under the 30th of Geo. 2, and is clearly and unequivocally a fraud, if the pretence made ufe of by Mr. Semple could be proved falfe; yet the *omus probandi* being thrown by law on Mr. Bayley, it would be next to im-poffible for him to prove that the Major had not left his pocket-book behind him, that he had not expended all his cafh, and that he was not going on a matrimonial expedition to Scotland to be united to a lady of large fortune.

Mr. Bayley, therefore, not being able to prove the *negative*, it was out of his power to put the Major to the trouble of proving the *affirmative*; (two words, by the bye, on which are founded every legal purfuit, and every fpecies of art and chi-canery in the profecution of it) he took the only remedy he had to try to recover his property; and no doubt very reluctantly, for we have every rea-

fon

son to think, that had Mr. Bayley had it in his power
to have proceeded otherwise, he would gladly
have relinquished the profecution in the shape of a
debt, and done justice to his country by adopting a
profecution for a *fraud*.

We are in possession also of another, but a still
more ingenious, adventure of his, in an excursion
from the north to town. He came to an inn on
the road in a post-chaise; and it being about two
o'clock, P. M. he said it was too soon for dinner,
but whilst the landlord was roasting a fowl, he
would amuse himself by viewing the church, &c.

The fowl was accordingly spitted; but it happening that the boy who drove Mr. Semple to the
above inn; had a sweetheart in the same place, he
left his horses to the care of the hostler, whilst he
went to pay his respects to his Dulcinea, at the
farther end of the town.

As the driver was standing at the door talking
with the lady, he saw a post-chaise coming along;
and having the curiosity to see who was therein,
was very much surprised to find the gentleman he
had just sat down at one inn, in a post-chaise belonging to another. But what appeared still more
surprizing was, he had not received his master's
fare; and, what was still worse, his own customary
compliment. It was in vain for the Major to draw
back and secrete himself. The boy ran back to
the inn, and told the circumstance, when the master
ordered two horses to be saddled; and, at the end of

two

wo ftages, the landlord and boy accofted Mr. Semple very rudely indeed, and infifted on his going before a magiftrate.

When they arrived at his worfhip's, the complaint was formally laid; and the Major being afked what he had to fay for himfelf, he ran through his lineage and hiftory, even from the year 1547, when the title of Lord Vifcount Lifle became extinct, to the very hour in which he was bade to to tell it; leaving out all the hair-breadth efcapes, difafters, chances, &c.

Having done this, with his ufual audacity and with equal hauteur he harangued on his importance to government. He declared himfelf the bofom friend of Mr. Pitt; faid he was on his Majefty's fervice with expreffes of the moft important and ferious nature to this kingdom; that he had exhaufted all his cafh; that he would compel every innkeeper on the road to furnifh him with horfes and chaife; and dared the magiftrate or landlord to moleft or detain him.

The authoritative ftile and manner in which he delivered himfelf, and the production of his *corps de referve,* Mr. Pitt's letters, produced an effect, that not only anfwered his utmoft purpofe, but produced more, much more, than Mr. Semple expected.

The magiftrate, whofe good wifhes towards government greatly inclined him to favour every thing that had the leaft fmack of it, was determined not to put a fpoke into the wheels of it. He took

K Mr.

Mr. Semple, therefore, into his private room, and not only told him he would pay the chaife, but actually offered him a fufficient fum of money to enable him to come to town; which offer the Major accepted, with a profufion of acknowledgments, and purfued his journey. And thus ended an exploit, which we difmifs without a comment. One fact we muft take notice of: the landlord was by far better off than the juftice; he was not only paid for his chaife, but the fowl, and even for the two poft-horfes which were ufed in the purfuit; whilft the other never knew where or how to recover a fhilling. The poftboy, however, with a crown in one hand, and his hat in the other, with a very low bow heartily wifhed his honor a good journey to London.

A circumftance which happened during the courfe of Mr. Semple's lucubrations, between his fervant and the lady to whom Mr. S. thought proper, *pro tempore*, to lend that name, may not be altogether unentertaining; at leaft it will vary the fcene, and afford a relaxation from that continual ftring on which we have already for a confiderable time fo very loudly thrummed.

In page 45, we mentioned his being at Mr. Carelefs's, White Hart, Watford. It was there that the gentlewoman who made ufe of the name of Semple, and every other name which the gentleman of that name had occafionally complimented her with, was detected in an amour with her own

ferving

ferving man, John Winter, by no lefs a perfonage
than the Major himfelf. The confequence was a
mutual difcharge of manual compliments and fervices. The lady knelt for forgivenefs, and the
Major's tendernefs granted it.

But this was not all that attended Mr. Semple
there; his unlucky ftars diftreffed him ftill further. His bag and baggage were detained by Mr.
Carelefs, and conveyed into the hands of Sir
Sampfon Wright: letters from Mr. Pitt, &c. &c.
were difcovered, with a pile of others, that made
Offa like a wart. They have been tranfmitted into
the hands of Lord Sydney, the fecretary of ftate,
and we are afraid, for ever irretrievable; unlefs
it fhould be thought proper, in mercy to mankind, to fuffer a hiftory to be publifhed, which
would aftonifh the world.

When we make ufe of fo large an expreffion as
the world, we do not mean to confine ourfelves
to a circumference of three miles, as Goldfmith's
midwife did, who had never been farther in her life,
had lain all the farmer's wives in that circle, and
boafted of her knowledge of the world; nor do we
mean a circle of a little larger magnitude, viz. that
of Great Britain and our town of Berwick-upon-
Tweed; but we mean an extent ftill more fpa-
cious, which the following letter will beft explain.

Spa,

SPA, July 4, 1786.

SIR,

ON my return to this place from Pruſſia, I ſhould think myſelf negligent did I not convey my reſpects to you by the earlieſt intelligence, and to acquaint you that I ſuffered much in my health, which I thank God is now much improved, no thanks to the party that occaſioned it. I have been at Bonn on the Rhine; and if the infamous S——— is ever ſeen there again, he is a priſoner for life, as he is more notorious in that place than in London, and THROUGHOUT THE CONTINENT. Mr. Heathcote has detained the carriage, and put his arms on it, and the banker has got both his cloaths and mine.

When at Bonn, Lambert's father and mother were unhappy beyond expreſſion relative to the boy. If you could give me the leaſt hint of him to ſatisfy the parents, you would do them a ſingular piece of charity.

I am, Sir,

Your moſt devoted humble ſervant,

JOHN WINTER.

The

The reader will excufe us putting the addrefs as we have not the confent of the gentleman fo to do.

Mr. Heathcote, the gentleman mentioned in the above letter, is refident from the Englifh court; and, according to the cuftom of the country, feized the carriage, for the ufe of thofe to whom it more properly belonged.

At Hamburgh, he contrived to get himfelf introduced to Mr. Matthias, the envoy; and by the means of that introduction to recommend himfelf to Mr. Matthias, in Scotland-yard, treafurer to her Majefty. Mr. J. G. Semple accompanied Mr. Matthias one evening to Covent-Garden houfe; and under pretence of having changed his breeches, and left his purfe behind him, he obtained five guineas of Mr. Matthias.

It would not have been extraordinary had this matter refted fingly; but on fome other pretence he obtained an equal fum of the fame gentleman.

Being at Egham, he contrived to make himfelf acquainted with Dr. Ogilvie, a very worthy divine of that place; and having fo done, and found by that means the tradefmen and others with whom the doctor dealt, Mr. Semple obtained credit of various people, Having alfo been feen arm in arm with the doctor at Windfor, wherever the latter went into a fhop the Major went afterwards, and got goods of fome and cafh of others.

Of

Of Mr. Gulliver, of the Duke's-Head, Belfont, near Hounflow, he obtained the fum of 10l. and gave Mr. Gulliver the fame valuable fecurity for it, as he had before given to Mr. Bailey, of Hope. But, in order to convince the reader that there could be no external appearance of poverty, we muft tell him, that the Major cut a dafh at Belfont; for he had fervants in livery, and a carriage which he called his own; but he never thought proper to put up at the Duke's-Head after the above affront beftowed on him by Mr. Gulliver, when Mr. Semple ufurped the name of Major Cunningham.

But his ingenuity was not fo circumfcribed as to be limited to feafts upon gentlemen who do not know the world: the gentlemen of the law, who are fuppofed to know moft of it, experienced his addrefs in the art of extracting gold out of the purfe.

Mr. Gapper, of the Temple, accommodated him with forty pounds; and Mr. Parker, of Hallifax, with fifty.

He was not, however, quite fo fuccefsful with Mr. Bell, bookfeller, of the Strand: under pretence of being employed by the miniftry, he applied for a confiderable fum of money, for conveying intelligence for the ufe of the Morning Poft; adding, he was going on an embaffy with difpatches to Germany, intrufted to him by Lord Shelburne, which contained a fecret negociation with the Emperor.

In

In this inſtance he was not quite a match for Mr. Bell; but in a few days after, when that gentleman was out, he called at the ſhop, and borrowed half a guinea, pretending he was arreſted. The Major's honour ſtill ſtands unredeemed at Mr. Bell's. It turned out, however, that Mr. Semple advanced the truth; for he was then actually in the cuſtody of Mr. Charles Hyndes, officer to the ſheriff of Middleſex.

Mr. Vincent, of Speenham-land, Newbury, Berks, has alſo authorized us to inſert the following application of Major Semple to that gentleman.

The Major arrived at Newbury about the month of March laſt, in a travelling chariot, and two ladies with him, and put up at the Pelican. There, alſo, he pretended that he had been ſo unlucky as to leave his pocket-book behind him at London, and that his caſh being expended, he was diſabled either to proſecute his journey to Bath, or return to town.

He enquired of the maſter of the inn whether there were not ſome of the military quartered there, and on his being informed that the Oxford Blues lay at Newbury, Mr. Semple made his pretended diſtreſs known to an officer or two of that corps, who declined to accommodate him, having, perhaps, travelled as far north as the Major.

On this he enquired for an army agent, but none being there, he aſked for ſome gentleman of character and reſpect, to whom he could make his
fituation

situation known. The waiter conducted him to Mr. Vincent's, who generously lent him five guineas, for which the Major gave his obligation, and took his leave with a profusion of grateful acknowledgments.

On his return, which was in a few days, instead of calling and discharging so honourable a debt, he gave himself the trouble of sending a note, with an apology, to Mr. Vincent, but took care to dispatch it just on the eve of his departure from Newbury, so that Mr. Vincent should not be under the necessity of troubling the Major with his personal appearance at the Pelican.

One little incident happened when the Major made his entré to Mr. Vincent, that may not be thought unworthy notice. On his mentioning his name, Mrs. Vincent asked him, ' Simple, did you ' say, Sir?' ' No, Madam,' replied he, ' not ' Simple, at your service, but Semple, a relation ' of Lord Semple's, and a Major in the Russian ' service.' On his departure Mrs. Vincent observed, that her husband perhaps might be *Simple*, but she was sure the fellow was no *Major*; which justifies a former observation, that the fair sex see into a sharper with much keener eyes than that philosophical animal called man.

Since the first appearance of these Memoirs, the Major, in one of his papers, complained of his offences being exaggerated, and denied any knowedge of Mr. Wood. Mr. Wood has, however,

con-

confirmed the facts fince; as has Mr. Tatterfal likewife; part of the tranfactions with that gentleman as ftated here, he alfo endeavoured to controvert. If the Major has now a fingle friend left, and that friend is poffeffed of common fenfe, he will recommend it to him to reft quiet, with the confolation of having efcaped the difgraceful exit of many better men, not a fiftieth part fo criminal.

The partiality which a candid and difcerning public ever beftows on induftrious merit, has enabled us to add full as many more anecdotes to that very numerous collection we have already compiled ; indeed, the fund feems to be inexhauftible.

In return for fo fingular a mark of its approbation, we fhall labour to preferve their countenance and protection; on the one hand, expreffing our gratitude, on the other, rejoicing in a defeat of thofe drones of literature, who perpetually prey on the honey collected with labour, and manufactured with the care and induftry of others. To the proof.

In the month of June laft Mr. Semple made his appearance at that fafhionable place of refort, the Wells of Buxton, in the neighbourhood of the Peak of Derby.

He came there in a ftyle that portrayed a perfon of fafhion. He had his Valet de Chambre, his *own* carriage, i. e. fpeaking more properly, the

L   carriage

carriage of Mr. Lycett, with two poſtillions, to whom he threw a crown each, and beſpoke a ſuite of apartments.

The arrival of this ſplendid ſtranger, who aſſumed all the airs and graces of a man of quality, ſtruck a panic in the minds of the ſquires of the Peak. Gentlemen of faſhion were ſmitten with envy, and the boſoms of the ſofter ſex palpitated with the hope of making a conqueſt of a man of ſuch figure and apparent fortune.

To increaſe his conſequence, he ſtyled himſelf the heir apparent of the dormant title of Lyſle; and, in order to lay the foundation for the completion of his purpoſe, in his journey to Buxton, Mr. Semple gave a ball to the ladies. We muſt obſerve here however, that it was part of Mr. Biſhop's caſh (vide page 57,) which enabled him to ſhine ſo conſpicuouſly at this bread-and-butter manufactory.

There was not a gentleman that did not court Mr. Semple's company, nor a lady that did not prick up her ears at the ſound of his name. He was accommodated with hunters, his own having, as he ſaid, been left at Loughborough.

This conſequence laſted about a week, when a ruſtic clergyman, who had more blunt honeſty about him than moſt of the refined gentleman there, began to ſuſpect the Major.——We call him Major, becauſe it was the title he there aſſumed, with the

Order

Order of Merit at his button-hole, which her Imperial Majesty of All the Ruffias had, he boasted, conferred on him for services done her.——

This clergyman, who, if any little tale of scandal chanced to reach his ears, was sure to propagate it, in order, as we suppose, to make mankind ashamed of their vices, was paid as much respect to out of the pulpit as, perhaps, he was in it, i. e. the place was too polite to give credit to a single syllable he said.

He chanced to have a very fine hunter or two, which Major Semple wished to purchase; but, as the latter did not haggle about the price, and offered to give his drafts on his London Banker, the clergyman in the warmth of his zeal for morality, thought proper to whisper to every person at Buxton that the Major was, *ad rem* to all intents and purposes, a swindler.

Had a notorious gambler but hinted half as much, there would not have been a moment's hesitation about the truth of it; but, as it was a clergyman that set the rumour abroad, it was debated whether he should not be sent to Coventry for a scandal-monger, and for picking holes in every man's cloth but his own.——

It happened, however, one morning, that he drew ten guineas out of a gentleman's purse, when they were out on a ride, pretending he had

L 2   accidentally

accidentally left his purfe at the inn, on the table; but he never afterwards took any notice about refunding it. This little incident, coupled with the clergyman's account, made a complete ftory, fo that when the Major made his next appearance, there were many long faces and fhy looks.

Mr. Semple was quick enough of comprehenfion to difcern it.—He accofted the ladies, and drank tea with them, with all the effrontery and nonchalance of firft-rate impudence. His prudence was as great as his comprehenfion. He ordered horfes to be put to the carriage, and carried his fword in his hand about the room for upwards of four hours, before he departed.

To wind up this excurfion, we muft inform our readers, that Lor Suffield, (late Sir Harbord Harboard) was then at Buxton. To that gentleman he pretended, that he had travelled with young Mr. Harbord in many places on the continent; but owned it was rather a delicate point to mention, that he had accommodated him in the route with a trifle of money, and defired Sir Harbord would acquaint him whether he fhould prefent the fmall account then, or wait the young gentleman's return.—On Sir Harbord's defiring to know the fum, and expreffing his obligations to him for having fupplied his fon with cafh abroad, Major Semple fat down, and foon produced a regular

account

account from ftage to ftage, amounting in the whole 'to thirty-fix guineas, which Sir Harbord paid him immediately.

It was the next day but one that the Major decamped from Buxton.—What further fums he obtained has not yet come to our knowledge; many had obliged the Major, who are too much of gentlemen to deftroy the obligation by divulging it.

It ought not to be forgot, for the Major's credit, that he threw a guinea to each of the waiters, and one to the tea-woman, thereby leaving Buxton with fome eclat.

The following little town anecdote ferves to illuftrate his character, and the fruitfulnefs of his genius ftill further.

On the 26th of April laft, happening to be paffing through Berner's-ftreet, he obferved Lady M'C—y coming out of Mr. Bowyers's, the minature painter, aud go into her carriage.—In about half an hour afterwards he did Mr. Bowyer the favour to call and fee his pictures; at the fame time obferving that Lady M'C—y, whom he knew was getting her picture done (and who was, as he faid, one of his moft intimate acquaintances) had been kind enough to recommend him to Mr. B. to have his picture painted.—He then fixed to take the firft fitting the next day at eleven.—But upon getting into the

hackney

hackney-coach, which was waiting for him at the
door, he fortunately recollected he had only a 10*l.*
note in his pocket, and flew back to Mr. Bowyer
to acquaint him with it, and requeſt the favour of
four or five ſhillings to pay for his coach, which he
meant preſently to diſcharge.—Mr. Bowyer complied with his requeſt, and upon Lady M'C—y's
coming to fit to Mr. Bowyer the next day, he
thanked her ladyſhip kindly for her recommendation of Col. George; but her ladyſhip could not
for the foul of her recollect the Colonel, or ever
hearing of his name before, who, in the midſt
of his great hurry of buſineſs, and very numerous engagements, forgot to take the fitting according to appointment; and Mr. Bowyer has
ſince thought himſelf extremely happy the Colonel
did not aſk for a much larger ſum.

At Norwich we have the following very ſingular
circumſtance, in which he was aſſiſted by the perſon who appeared there as the Major's Lady.—

Among others with whom he ingratiated himſelf
was Dr. M'Quin, at whoſe houſe the Major and
his Lady lodged, by invitation, (as the noiſe of the
inn was offenſive to madam) in nearly the ſame
ſtyle and faſhion he had before done at Buxton.—
And ſuch was his diſſipation, that though he was
daily reduced to the ſhifts of robbing, to ſupport
it, yet no ſooner was he in poſſeſſion of a ſmall
ſum,

fum, than he was as induſtrious to ſquander it, and rely on his invention for further ſupplies.

He had borrowed five guineas of the Doctor, and had diſſipated it in a ball, by which he had incurred the Doctor's diſpleaſure, he being a gentleman who knew the value of money too well, to throw it away in a manner ſo totally vague and empty, and without conferring any one good to ſociety by it.——

In a ſhort time after he applied again to the Doctor for the ſum of fifteen guineas, and then offered his draft on his agent in town. To this application Dr. M'Quin was very averſe, took the liberty of rallying the Major on the lightneſs of his conduct, and expatiated on the ill effects it muſt naturally produce. To this expoſtulation Major Semple pleaded the appendages of a gentleman's life, and argued how neceſſary thoſe little ſuperfluities were to ſupport the character which birth, education, and cuſtom, claimed as rights hereditary.

In this argument it was that the lady gave an inſtance of her ingenuity, which by no means diſparaged her paramour's choice ; for, on the Doctor's declining to lend the fifteen guineas, the ſhock her nerves ſuſtained was ſo great as quite to overcome that delicacy of feeling which generous and liberal minds muſt feel at a pecuniary repulſe. In ſhort, ſhe ſwooned, or rather ſeemed to ſwoon away, when her ſittuation apparently required all
the

the little offices of hartfhorn, water, &c. &c. and made the Doctor and his lady feel as much real concern as if the fit had been real.

When Mrs Semple was able to open her eyes, and glance them towards her dear Major, fhe by degrees opened her mouth, and gently chid him for the application; and giving him her keys, defired he would go up ftairs and take three diamond pins to difpofe of, which would produce five times the fum required, and might be eafily replaced in London.

The fituation of the lady, her apparent diftrefs of mind, the agitations that the Major was in on her account, and her fo readily offering to difpofe of her diamonds for the Major's ufe, made fuch an impreffion on the Doctor, that he relaxed from his firft refolution, and inftantly fetched the money, of which he now intreated the Major's acceptance.

Strange as this may feem, it will turn out a little ftranger ftill; the reader may recollect a circumftance that happened at Mr. Carelefs's, at Watford, with the above lady and her fervant.— The fcene was renewed at Dr. M'Quin's, the lady being obferved to come out of the footman's room in her fhift: as foon as the Doctor was apprifed of it, he difcharged the groupe, without the fatisfaction of being paid either the twenty guineas

or

or the lodging, happy, no doubt, to get rid of guests who were a difgrace to the roof that afforded them a fhelter, and a plague to every perfon with whom they were acquainted.

Dr. M'Quin, however, was not the only fufferer at Norwich.—Mr. Pye, a taylor, was one of thofe unfortunate tradefmen who gave credit to appearances, and of whom Mr. Semple has, for a confiderable number of years, made a conftant prey.— Indeed, without a taylor no man can appear like a gentleman : the equipments of the head and heart may have fome trifling confideration with a few unfafhionable fellows, but a knave in embroidery has always the countenance and fupport of the *beau monde.* The advantages he derived from his lodging at Dr. M'Quin's, he took care to purfue with the eagernefs of a thorough-bred gamefter. Having made ufe of the ufual artifice of drawing a letter from the Doctor, and having alfo made his way to Colonel Debbeig, who was a particular friend of Dr. M'Quin's, by producing that letter, and urging his intimacy, he obtained five guineas from the Colonel.

The Major affumed alfo his ufual modefty on the occafion, by foliciting foon after the fum of five more; but which were pofitively refufed him, through the circumfpective eye of the Colonel's lady, who faw a little more into the Major than the Colonel; and by her advice it was that her

M   hufband

hufband was a fufferer for the fum of five guineas only.—

By a fimilar pretence he got fix guineas of Captain Seaton, at Thirfk, in Yorkfhire; but with Dr. Aiken, of Yarmouth, he was a little more fuccefsful, for that gentleman generoufly offered, and the Major as readily accepted, the fum of twenty pounds.

An innkeeper at the laft mentioned place, whofe name we have not yet learnt, was ftill a greater fufferer than Dr. Aiken, for at that inn he borrowed twenty-five pounds, which, like the reft of the Major's borrowings, ftill remains unpaid.

Of Mr. De Roman, hatter to the Duke de Orleans, in St. James's-ftreet, he obtained a fine riding-hat and feather for his lady, and a *chapeau à la Ruffe* for himfelf; pretending he was in the Emprefs's fervice.—At this period the Major lived in Bond-ftreet.—Though the reader muft, by this time, be tolerably well convinced, that Mr. Semple's affurance did not ftick at trifles, yet he can fcarcely imagine that he had effrontery fufficient to conduct himfelf to the table of the Marquis of Lanfdown, then Lord Shelburne.—This, however, is the fact; he not only dined, but was intrufted with difpatches, to carry abroad, by the Marquis.

We are ftill ftrangers to the means by which he introduced himfelf, but we have it from unqueftionable authority, that he referred the Marquis to a gentleman of the Temple for his character; for

the

the character of which gentleman the Marquis was referred to the Master of the Rolls; whose *report* was to the following effect: *"That if Major Semple was a friend of Mr. G——d's, there could be no diffi- culty made about employing him."*

It was in consequence of this enquiry and report that Mr. Semple was intrusted with dispatches to Vienna; which he shamefully neglected: they lay at Mr. G——d's a considerable time, and were afterwards removed to Mr. Careless's at Watford; from whence, with two others, they were transmitted to Sir Sampson Wright, who, as before mentioned, delivered them to the Secretary of State.

The adage is old, but not less true, " that great " wits have short memories:"—That Mr. Semple lived by his wits, few will be bold enough to deny; and that a man who can, for a number of years, live daily by them, must be a great wit, there are very few but will allow. Having, by this kind of reasoning, established the *Major*, we come to prove the con- clusion, his short memory.

It was at one of the foregoing hours of inter- course, viz. at dinner, that Mr. Semple gave a glaring proof of the shortness of his memory. The subject turned on politics, and at last came to the late peace, when Mr. Semple, with all that vacuity of thought and absence of mind, which so often distinguishes great wits, took occasion to observe, *" That it was the most damned peace that ever " was made."*

The

The Marquis's fork, which was on the tip of his lip, with a morsel of chicken on the point of it, was, with hand and arm suspended thereon.—He stared at the Major, the Major stared at the Marquis, who, in a few seconds, ejaculated, " Sir !" to which the other replied, " My lord !"—" I beg " your pardon," said the Marquis, " I thought, " Sir, you called for a glass of wine." " Oh, no, my " Lord," replied Mr. Semple, " I said it was the " most damned peace that ever was made."— " Then I'll help you to a good one," answered the Marquis; and immediately began to load the Major's plate, meaning, no doubt, it was high time for him to stop his mouth.

The great art of living *with* the world is, to accommodate our opinions to those of our company;—to fathom their inclinations, their prejudices, their passions, and assimilate our own thereby, in proportion even to their moral as well as political barometer, else we can never meet with the good opinion of our equals, or the countenance of our superiors.—When we say this, we mean to regulate our opinion by the natural depravity of mankind.

The fact will speak for itself better than a thousand comments. From that hour Mr. Semple never sat down to table with the Marquis; and whenever he called on business was sure to wait a most considerable time before his name could even be be announced, but much more so ere he could gain an audience.

The late Dr. Goldfmith (the good-natured reader will readily pardon the comparifon) made once a fimilar blunder with the very felf-fame great per-fonage,—They both happened to be in the ftage-box of Covent Garden Theatre one evening, when the Doctor, who was then a ftranger, was intro-duced to his Lordfhip. The latter profeffed himfelf exceedingly happy; was honoured by the Doctor's company, and invited him to fupper, which was ac-cepted. However, in the courfe of the converfa-tion at the Theatre, his Lordfhip obferved, that the Public-papers had given him the appellation of Malagrida, but for what reafon he could not dif-cover.—Nor I neither, faid the Doctor, for every body knows that Malagrida was a very honeft man.—

This abrupt and uncourtly wit loft the Doctor a fupper, and the honour of his Lordfhip's good opi-nion, who never fpoke to him during the remainder of the entertainment, or took notice of him at part-ing.—

But, anecdote and wit apart, we muft confefs that there is fomething fo atrocioufly mean and bafe in the character of a SWINDLER, that it were to be wifhed fwindling was made a capital offence.—The highwayman ranks very low, indeed, in the fcale of criminality, when compared to the fwindler, be-caufe he is oftentimes urged by motives which

excite

excite our pity and compaſſion, whilſt he hazards his life; but the ſwindler is a wretch, who ignobly exiſts by taking advantages of the generous credulity, and thoſe amiable weakneſſes of human nature which are the ornament of mankind.

In the courſe of the laſt year we trace our gentleman to a lodging at the Leaping-Bar, over Black Friar's Bridge, where he had retired from the noiſe and buſtle which his conſequence had occaſioned at the court end of the town.

It was at this place that his good genius afforded him an opportunity to carry into execution a ſcheme of a more, if we may be allowed the expreſſion, raſcally nature than any he had hitherto practiſed.

The hair-dreſſer waiting on him one morning, Mr. Semple ſeemed angry that the maſter did not attend him; for which neglect the journeyman apologized, by ſaying, his maſter would have come, but he was getting ready for a journey to Scotland.—To Scotland! ſaid Mr. Semple, what part is he going to? To Edinburgh, Sir, replied the journeyman.— And pray what ſort of a man is your maſter, and how does he dreſs?— Oh, Sir, anſwered the frizzeur, he is a very good looking man, and dreſſes quite genteel.——Then tell him, ſaid Semple, that he is exceedingly lucky, for I am going to Edinburgh, and will take him with me in my chaiſe. But what is his name? Kerr, anſwered anfwered the journeyman.——Then, faid Semple, fend Mr. Kerr to me inftantly.

The man departed for his mafter, who immediately waited on the Major. Matters were foon fettled, and off they went that very evening — Mr. Kerr rejoicing at the good luck he had met with, and Mr. Semple congratulating himfelf on the good luck he expected to meet.

In this happy difpofition of mind they travelled till they came to York, but when there, a little circumftance occurred, at which Major Semple feemed very much hurt. Before dinner, he went out, and in half an hour returned, expreffing much uneafinefs at a trick that had been played him in town. He had lent a gentleman, a friend of his, he faid, a fum for which that friend had given him a draught on his banker at York; but when he prefented it, the banker had no cafh of that gentleman's in his hand, and declined honouring the draft.

This, Mr. Semple faid, was exceedingly unlucky, as he had relied on that gentleman's bill to carry him forward; but, added he, Mr. Kerr, you perhaps have fome gold about you. O yes, Sir, anfwered Mr. Kerr, I have fifteen guineas.—Then, faid Semple, let me have them, and when we come to Edinburgh I will repay you.

Mr.

He Mr. Kerr readily gave Mr. Semple the fifteen guineas, and away they went again; nothing material occurring till they came within half a mile of Edinburgh, when Mr. Semple said, he should walk, as he wanted to call on a nobleman, *him* desired Mr. Kerr to go to Fortune's Coffee-house, and he would be with him in half an hour at farthest.

He Mr. Kerr went to Fortune's; and to make short of the story, that half hour has never yet arrived.—Happily he had some friends in Edinburgh, to whom he related his story, and who supplied him with the needful, or he must have been left in a situation which none can know but those who are ashamed to borrow, too proud to beg, and too honest to steal.

With the master of Brown's Coffee-house, Mitre Court, he played off the following curious device. Having run a bill for a few pounds, and decamped without recollecting that circumstance, he was seen, some time after, sitting in a hackney-coach, near Mitre Court, by a little girl, the daughter of one of the porters of the Temple, to whom Mr. Semple was indebted a few shillings.

The child recognizing Mr. Semple, she ran and told her father;—the father ran and told the master of the coffee-house, and both ran to the coach.—In vain were all Mr. Semple's apologizes and promises,

mifes, nothing but prompt payment would do with
them; and finding that words would not be fatisfactory, he defired them to meet him at the Treafury, where he fhould fee fome of his friends,
either Mr. Pitt, Dr. Prettyman, or Mr. Rofe,
who, the Major faid, were greatly in arrear with
him, on government account, and then he would
fatisfy the bill and the porter.—

The bait, however, did not take, for they not
only refufed to give him a meeting at the Treafury,
but rudely infifted on accompanying him in the
coach; and ftepping in, away they drove to the
Treafury; where, after Mr. Semple had traverfed
the rooms, with his companions clofe at his heels,
and found his foregoing friends bufy about other government accounts, and therefore invifible, as the
Major called it, he then propofed taking them to
his relation, Lord Rawdon, in St. James's Place,
where he could have any cafh he wanted.

Away they drove to Lord Rawdon's, and ftopped
within a few doors of it. The Major left them
in the coach, and went to his Lordfhip's houfe,
where he knocked with as much, or more, rapi-
dity than the owner of it would have done, and
was inftantly admitted.

The gentlemen left in the coach, having waited
near an hour, and beginning to grow impatient,
they went with an humble tap at his Lordfhip's;
and, in a quarter of an hour, were anfwered to the
following effect:—That a gentleman had come in,

N   whe

who called himſelf a relation of his Lordſhip's, ſaid he was purſued by Bailiffs, and prayed to be let through the houſe into the Green Park, which had accordingly been done, out of pity to a great man in diſtreſs.

A proper explanation ſoon took place, to the no ſmall diverſion of the family ; and though the maſter of the coffee-houſe had three ſhillings and ſix-pence coach-hire to pay, he could not refrain from joining in the humour.

We are in poſſeſſion of numerous other tricks of a ſimilar nature, but ſhall conclude with the following ones :

The Major lately lodged in Mitre Court, and on a Sunday evening he went to Meſſrs. Butts and Hand, in Fleet-ſtreet, where he had before laid out a trifle, and thereby was known, and pretended that a friend of his had been arreſted for a tolerable large ſum of money ; that ſome gentlemen had contributed to diſcharge the debt, and the whole that was wanting to make up the ſum was thirty-ſix ſhillings ; that having nothing but an hundred pound note about him, which was very difficult on ſuch a day to get changed, he requeſted the loan of that ſum till the morrow, when he would return it.

Motives of compaſſion prevailed over prudence.
—The Major obtained the money, and *the morrow*, like his *half-hour* with Mr. Kerr, has never yet arrived.

We

We have been favoured also with the following anecdotes of Mr. Semple when in Ruſſia. Vide the beginning of this Narrative.

By the recommendation of the Dutcheſs of Kingſton * he came to Peterſburgh, and by her intereſt he obtained the rank of Aid-de camp to Prince Potemkin, and with that General went to the Crimea.——On Mrs. Semple's writing to her huſband, complaining of the Dutcheſs of Kingſton's ſlighting her, he returned to Peterſburgh, and by a great deal of bluſter ſo frightened her, that he obliged the Dutcheſs, before he left the houſe, to give him five hundred roubles, (about three and ſix-pence each;) he ſtaid afterwards in Peterſburgh; but before he left the place ſold his carriage to four different Ruſſian noblemen; took the caſh of every one of them, and promiſed to ſend the carriage to each.

His method of getting out of the country was as follows:—He was accuſtomed to walk out at the gate of Narve, on the frontiers of Poland, with a ſervant carrying his great coat, and after his walk to return; but one day his memory failed him, and he never came back. It muſt be obſerved, that no ſtranger can leave the Ruſſian dominions

* Major Semple's diſtreſſes were impreſſed on the mind of the Dutcheſs of Kingſton by her Secretary, Mr. Lilly, in the firſt inſtance; for which ſervice, and many other acts of kindneſs, the Major very gratefully ſwindled Mr. Lilly out of a gold watch, and thirty guineas in money.

N 2　　　　　　　without

without giving notice three times in the public-papers, or obtaining a pass from the General of the Police, which must be counter-signed at the Admiralty.

He also swindled a Ruffian officer out of a rich regimental suit, by the following stratagem: He met him at court, and begged he would let his (Semple's) taylor look at the suit of clothes, to make some like it, in order to bring to England. The credulous officer delivered them to Semple's servants, but never saw them after.

When he first appeared at Saint Petersburgh he called himself at the English Tavern Lord Semple, and his company was courted by every body.—What is remarkable, he was presented to the Emprefs in an highland dress, and esteemed by Prince Potemkin as an excellent soldier.

Before we dismiss the subject of his behaviour at Ruffia, we cannot help observing, that with the high recommendation of the Dutchefs, the favour in which he stood with the Emprefs, the estimation in which he was held by Prince Potemkin as a soldier, and by all persons of fashion at Saint Peterfburgh, as a gentleman, it was impoffible but he must have acquired an immenfe fortune, and been distinguished with the highest military honours, had not a natural propensity to dishonesty superseded every moral and self-consideration.

As the 7th edition was going to press, the Editor of these Memoirs received the following facts from a friend whom he can rely upon.

SIR,

AS you are publishing a series of editions, relative to the life and rogueries of Major Semple, I beg leave to inclose you a few of his singular tricks, to insert in a future edition; they are literally true.

I am, Sir,

your obliged servant,

Oct. 14, 1786.

" In the month of January, a Mr. D———
was sitting with some friends in the Treasury
Coffee-house, Whitehall, and perceiving a person
in an opposite box, whose features he thought were
familiar to his memory, ventured to accost him, and
found, upon a mutual explanation, that his name
was *George Semple*, who had formerly been his
school-fellow at Edinburgh: as Scotchmen upon
the recognition of old acquaintance constantly enquire into the situation of each other, Mr. D———
                                        questioned

queſtioned Major Semple as to his purſuits in life, and received for information, that he had ſpent a conſiderable part of his time abroad, but the *climate* not agreeing with his *conſtitution*, he had thought it *expedient* to return to England, where he had formed acquaintance with ſome perſons of the firſt rank, among whom were Col. St. Leger, and Sir John St. Aubin; and that the former had the day before introduced him to the Prince of Wales, who was ſo ſtruck with his accompliſh- ments, that he promiſed him every ſervice in his power; he told his friend D—— that he was en- gaged to dinner on that particular day with a party of the officers of the guards at the Saint James's Coffee-houſe, but ſhould be happy to meet him on the following day at the Treaſury Coffee-houſe, to eat a bit of mutton, and rehearſe the pranks of their boyiſh hours; according to this intimation, Mr. D—— provided a dinner, and the Major came, agreeable to appointment. In the courſe of their converſation, the diſhonourable ſubject of theſe memoirs did not fail to aſſure Mr. D—— of uſing his intereſt in the circles of faſhion to the advantage of his friend. Mr. D—— was grateful for his good wiſhes, and was in the act of returning the Major thanks, when their diſcourſe was inter- rupted by the ſervant entering with a note to the ingenious principal of this narrative; the contents were inſtantly communicated to Mr. D——, by which he learned, that a friend of the Major's

. was

was waiting for him at the British Coffee-house in Cockfpur-ftreet, from whom he expected the loan of two hundred pounds, but being fhort of cafh, intreated his friend D— to lehd him what cafh he had about him; that he would difcharge the expences of the dinner, meet his friend at the coffee-houfe, and return without fail in the evening, when ten or twenty guineas fhould be at Mr. D——'s fervice; accordingly Mr. D—— lent the Major two guineas, and he departed on his embaffy to Cockfpur-ftreet. But guefs the furprife of Mr. D ——, who, when in the act of retiring, under the idea of the bill having been difcharged, was accofted by the mafter of the houfe with the account; he then underftood that the honeft Major had not only forgot to difcharge the bill, but had actually borrowed half a guinea from the maid-fervant of the coffee-houfe in the name of Mr. D——; it was fome weeks afterwards before Mr. D—— got a glimpfe of the impoftor, but accidentally meeting him in Titchfield-ftreet, he upbraided him in terms of great feverity for his behaviour; not fo much for the deceit practifed on himfelf, as for the mean and unworthy ufe he had made of his name, to rob a poor fervant of half a guinea. The Major received the admonitions of Mr. D—— with a fort of philofophic indifference, till finding he had to deal with a man of fpirit, he confented to walk with Mr. D—— to the coffee-houfe, and repay the money; but on

their

their arrival, the Major fwore he had but five fhillings in his purfe, which, unwillingly, he gave the girl, and Mr. D—— made up the remainder.

After this proof of *Semple's* contaminated principles, Mr. D—— kept him at a great diftance, and faw no more of him until one night about twelve o'clock, he heard a violent knocking at his door; on an enquiry into the caufe, he found it was the Major, wet to the fkin, who had walked all the way from the metropolis to Chelfea, to implore permiffion of his friend D—— to fleep upon his carpet, as he was deftitute of friends, money, or lodging; the compaffion of Mr. D—— overcame his refentment, and he complied with his prayer, but the Major repeated the requeft fo often in the courfe of the winter, that Mr. D——, from a too firmly grounded fufpicion of his honefty, was obliged peremptorily to forbid him his houfe and acquaintance for ever."

Having a good perfon, and handfome address, he generally fucceeded, without difficulty, in his infamous fchemes; however, notwithftanding he obtained the poffeffion of other peoples property with fo much facility, he was in fome refpects a great economift, and not unfrequently travelled two or three hundred miles in a poft-chaife and four horfes, at lefs expence than even a rider to a tradefman could on horfeback. His method was, to confult the different books of the roads which takes notice of the gentlemens feats

in

in every county, particularly thofe near the great or principal roads. As foon as he arrived at the end of a ftage, he always pretended fome bufinefs with a neighbouring nobleman or man of confequence, to whofe houfe he chofe to walk, but firft befpoke a dinner or fupper, according to the hour, at the inn to which the chaife of the laft ftage had brought him, informing the poftillions * he would be back before they could refrefh their horfes, at the fame time ordering another chaife to be ready at his return; thus, all doubts of his honour were effectually ftifled. His next ftep was to go to another inn at a diftance, or in another ftreet in the fame town or village, order a chaife in a hurry, whip into it, and proceed with the utmoft fpeed; whilft thofe he had duped were wondering he was detained fo long at the gentleman's whofe name he ufed:——— in time fufpicion commenced, and a perfon was difpatched to the houfe; the enquiry confirmed the cheat, as the meffenger of courfe learned he had not been there.

Thus, he is faid to have travelled at little or no expence, in the ftile of a gentleman, over three-fourths of the kingdom.

Another of his methods of travelling at the expence of others, was prefenting bills for large

* The Major much more frequently travelled with four, than two horfes.

fums,

fums, which the inn-keepers' feldom chofe to change, if they could.

At Leeds he put up at Mr. Wood's, the Old King's Arms, hired four poft and two faddle horfes, and offered a bill for 100*l.* which Mr. Wood could not, or did not choofe, to change.—He then told Wood, that he was going to Hull, on urgent bufinefs, and fhould be back in a few days, and borrowed three guineas of him. When the fix horfes were returned from Tadcafter, he paid nothing for hire, but defrauded him of his three guineas, horfe-hire, and reckoning.

It is, from very good authority, faid, that he travelled upon the fame plan all the way from Manchefter to Hull, continually offering his bill for exchange, and always wanted to borrow money till he returned.

In 1778, he was at Bury St. Edmunds, in Suf-folk, in the character of Captain Semple, where his performances were as follows:

He was at the Six Bells Inn fome time; never paid for board or lodging.

He took up a fuit of clothes of Mr. Spink, and never paid for them.

He borrowed a fum of money of Colonel Shutz, and never paid it.

At a fale of plate and other goods at Bury, he purchafed fome lots, and got the landlord to pay for them; he took the lots with him, but never repaid the landlord.

He

He was one night in company with —— Sylyard,
Efq; of Haughley, and faid he wanted to go to
town in the morning, and afked him for twenty
pounds; Mr. Sylyard lent him all the money he
had in his pocket, amounting to five guineas; he
gave him a note upon a pretended uncle at Edin--
burgh, but no fuch perfon was found. Mr. Sylyard has the note now.

He took in Mr. Woodward, the hatter, for a
new hat.

And Mr. Decke, bookfeller, the poft-mafter of
Bury, for a fet of books.

In the fpring of eighty-four he introduced himfelf to the officers mefs at Mr. Clode's, the White
Hart, at Windfor. On the third or fourth day of
his dining there, the Colonel, who had been
abfent in London, came down, and joined the corps
at dinner, where he prefided; the Major was introduced to him as a gentleman in the Emprefs of
Ruffia's fervice, and placed in the feat of honour,
viz. on the Colonel's right hand.

When dinner was nearly over, a young gentleman
belonging to the fame regiment entered, and, after
paying his refpects generally, was going to take his
chair, when the Colonel introduced him to Major
Semple; the moment he heard his name, and viewed
his perfon, he drew back, and addreffed himfelf to
the corps in thefe words:

" This Major Semple, as he is pleafed to call
" himfelf, looking full in his face, is an im-

Q 2   " poftor,

" poftor, a notorious fwindler, whom I faw pub-
" licly kicked when I was in Yorkfhire * laft
" fummer on a vifit to my friends." The company ftared at the Major, then at their friend,
who had fpoken with fo much freedom, but were
totally filent for a few feconds, waiting the Major's reply; at laft he recovered from his con-
fufion, and gave the lie direct to the bafe charge;
the young officer, quite confounded at his effrontery, and finding the company began to think
he was in an error, which the ftrong refem-
blance of perfons often occafions, became almoft
frantic; however, he prefently recollected that
the fame fervant, that attended him in Yorkfhire upon the above excurfion, was then be-
low; he immediately rang the bell, and ordered
the waiter to fend his fervant up, who happened to be an Irifhman; as foon as he entered, the Colonel, at his mafter's requeft, exa-
mined him.

Colonel. Did you attend your mafter to Yorkfhire
laft fummer ?

Servant. Indeed I did, your honour.

Colonel. Look round this company, and inform
me if you ever faw any of them in that part of the
country during the time you ftaid with your mafter.

* In the laft edition Leeds was mentioned as the place where
he was thus difgraced; but upon enquiry, that is not the
name of the town; the fact, however, is true.

Servant.

Servant. Faith I need not be long about that; sure I saw; I do not know what to call him, that person on your honour's right hand there; and he was pelted for a common cheat; upon my soul, after that I never expected to see him in such good company.

The Colonel having no longer any doubts, ordered the servant to walk up to the head of the table, and kick the Major out of the room; which he instantly did, without meeting with the least opposition.

During his visits at the White Hart, he agreed to give Mr. Clode fifty guineas for a very fine horse, formerly belonging to the Prince of Wales; however, Mr. Clode having some suspicion of the Major, sent a man and horse to dodge and seize him when he rode him out upon trial, in case he attempted to run away with the horse. The Major looked behind him several times, and perceiving the man constantly following him, suspected the cause, and for once kept his word, by returning the horse.

A Colonel C---*, who lived for some time in the neighbourhood of Staines, and our Major, were very intimate, and jointly performed several extraordinary manœuvres.

---

* This Colonel is also a noted swindler, and is, or has been lately, in confinement for debt.

Mr.

Mr. Styles, houfe-broker and brazier at Staines, lent Colonel C - - - fome furniture, under an agreement of fo much per month.

When Mr. Styles applied, at the ufual time, for payment, this valiant military pair of heroes beat the man, who had nothing to defend himfelf, moft unmercifully; even purfued him out of the houfe, and kicked him down the fteps. He however did, by great attention, and at fome expence, get part of his furniture back, but never recovered a fhilling of his bill.

Mr. Slark, of the fame town, a taylor, whom they employed, and who tried to get his money by feveral applications to the Colonel, they endeavoured to treat in a fimilar manner; but he was fortunate enough to efcape by the activity of his heels.

The Colonel run up a bill of upwards of forty pounds with Mr. Crawley, coal-merchant and corn-factor, at Staines, which he employed Mr. Robert Mackafon, an attorney in that neighbourhood, to recover for him. Here alfo our Major took an active part, and procured Jew bail for his worthy friend, by which Mr. Crawley loft the whole money and cofts. Mr. White, at the Bufh Inn at Staines, has furnifhed both the Colonel and Major with cafh, poft-chaife, and entertainments, to the amount of between forty and fifty pounds; not one fhilling of which he has ever been able to recover.

He

He took lodgings at a gentleman's houſe in the medical line, near Bloomſbury, where he had introduced himſelf as an old ſchool-fellow of his brother. One morning they walked into the city together; the gentleman's buſineſs led him into Mr, Stock's ſhop, a chemiſt, upon Lydgate-hill, late Mr. Dalmahoy's; where a general converſation took place for a few minutes; after which they went out together; however, the Major returned in a few minutes, apologized, as he had done to Butts and Hand, ſee page 106, viz. a friend of his was arreſted, but he had made up the whole ſum except three guineas, which he requeſted Mr. Stock would lend him, and it ſhould be repaid faithfully in a day or two; he ſucceeded, and had but juſt left the ſhop, when the gentleman returned to caution Mr. Stock not to give him credit in conſequence of the appearance of intimacy between them. However, the hint came too late; Mr. Stock has ſince declared, his manner had ſo totally removed all ſuſpicion of fraud, that he would have lent him twenty guineas, if he had aſked for ſo much.

Mr. Stock's account of his manner of obtaining the three guineas convinced the gentleman that it was neceſſary to get rid of his lodger directly: — as ſoon as he returned to his houſe, he went into the Major's apartment, where he found more proofs of his

his knavery—Two parcels of goods, with bills of parcels, *but no receipts*; particularly several pair of silk stockings; he did not stay for his lodger's return, but sent to the people who had furnished the goods, and returned them their property.

When the Major came home he was desired to provide new lodgings immediately; this order was accompanied by his landlord's declaration of his motives for acting in this precipitate manner. Semple seemed much confused at the discovery, but withdrew as he was directed.

A servant Semple had then with him owned to this gentleman, that his master had been in upwards of thirty different lodgings within four months.

Mr. Croft, mans-mercer and taylor, in Fleet-street, was rather fortunate; after having delivered a few clothes, for which he was not paid, he received a second order, for some very expensive articles. While they were making, he heard the Major's character by accident, and consequently has the goods now by him *. His transactions with Mr. Croft were in the name of Winter.

The Major lodged a short time before he was apprehended at Chelsea, where he formed an acquaintance with two gentlemen, who frequented the shop

* Amongst these clothes is an expensive singular coat, which renders it unsaleable; in this coat the Major intended to appear at court the last birth-day.

of Mr. Dickie, ftationer, in the Strand; he accompanied them there once or twice, and foon after came alone, and obtained a few prints and ftationary, promifing to pay for them next day, inftead of which, he called and made an excufe for borrowing half a guinea, which he received of Mrs. Dickie: he afterwards attempted to borrow five guineas, and obtain credit for a large travelling-cafe, with a filver lock; but Mr. Dickie having heard fomething of our Hero's tricks that morning, wifely kept his purfe fhut, and his travelling-cafe for a better pay-mafter.

Laft winter Semple happened to meet Mr. Grant, a very refpectable countryman of his, at the Opera-houfe. He entered into converfation upon variety of fubjects, in which he took care to mention his rank in the Ruffian army, his travels through different parts of Europe, and foon worked himfelf into Mr. Grant's good opinion. His firft attempt at this gentleman's purfe, was made as follows: He fent a porter to him, with a note, mentioning, that he had engaged to go an airing that morning in a balloon from the Lyceum; but owing to a difappointment the day before, he was ten pounds fhort of what he had agreed to give for this aerial voyage; that he could not think of afking credit of fuch people as he hired the balloon of, therefore would be obliged to him for that fum till the next day. Mr. Grant, having no

P   fufpicion

fufpicion of the honour of his new acquaintance, immediately fent him, under cover, a ten pound bank note. It is fcarcely neceffary to add, that the balloon-adventure, and the return of the ten pounds, agreeable to promife, are both in nubibus, as neither have yet happened.

In his morning vifits at Mr. Grant's apartments, he took notice of his hair-dreffer, a Mr. Walker, who keeps a perfume fhop in Saint James's Street, complimented him on his fuperiority in his art, and did him the favour to call upon him, and borrow, at different times, the fum of fix guineas, under a variety of pretences: Mr. Grant, finding the ten pounds were not returned at the time promifed, and the Major had alfo left off his ufual vifits, began to mention his fufpicions to Mr. Walker, who immediately took the alarm, and informed him of his having lent the fix guineas, with the manner in which he had obtained them. All doubt about him was now removed; they both agreed from that moment to exert themfelves in endeavouring to bring him to juftice, or recover their money; however, for fome time their efforts were in vain, at laft, Mr. Walker's man faw him accidentally ftop in a carriage in Duke's Street, Saint James's, and go into the houfe of a lady, whofe name we cannot upon this occafion (as will appear by the fequel) mention with propriety.

Mr.

Mr. Walker's man continued oppofite the houfe, to prevent his efcape, and employed a boy to go for his mafter, who, as foon as he arrived, hearing the bufinefs from his man, knocked at the door, and ran up ftairs. The Major difcovered great figns of fear, as well as furprize, hoped Mr. Walker, would forgive his breach of promife, and take his word once more, till he had returned from the Bank, where he declared he was then going in the carriage at the door, with the lady of the houfe, to receive fome money. Mr. Walker propofed going with him to the Bank, or where he pleafed, but would not upon any confideration part with him till he had his fix guineas, or carried him before a Magiftrate. The Major begged, prayed, and protefted he would not fleep before he paid him. It was all to no purpofe ; Mr. Walker was not to be moved. At laft, after the lady and the Major had held a long private converfation, he brought out of an inner apartment a filver tea-pot, as fecurity for the money ; this Mr. Walker accepted, and carried home. The next morning the Major called upon him, and obferving that the tea-pot was worth twice the debt, requefted Mr. Walker would lend him another guinea upon it ; which he refufed. However, he found a friend in the neighbourhood ; for though he then went away, he foon returned again with the money, and took away the pawn. The next morning, if not the fame after-

noon,

noon, the lady called to requeſt Mr. Walker would not part with the tea-pot but to her, as it was her property. When ſhe was informed of the Major's having redeemed it, ſhe immediately broke out into violent exclamations againſt him, ſaying, that villain had, under various pretences, almoſt ruined her. Without any comment upon this tranſaction, it is plain, neither connections, nor ſituations of the moſt delicate nature, could induce him to refrain from the moſt diſhonourable actions that ever diſgraced a profeſſed ſharper.

By intriguing with a ſervant, he got admiſſion to the town-houſe of William Brand, Eſq; of Polſted in Suffolk, while the family were abſent in the country. Here he eſtabliſhed his chief quarters for nearly two months, and derived all the credit which a very conſtant correſpondence with himſelf by letters in ſuch a ſituation could afford him. He made all the buſtle he could with his carriage in the neighbourhood, where he was ſuppoſed to have connection with Mr. Brand, and went by the name of the Handſome Major.

It was his conſtant practice to gain all the knowledge of peoples property poſſible. He ſoon found that a widow lady, who lived hard by was very rich. He called on her one morning in a great hurry. A bill of thirty guineas, he ſaid, had been preſented for payment, and he was at a loſs for caſh juſt at that moment.

He

He hoped she would excuse his applying to her, as it was on Mr. Brand's account, but he would certainly return her the cash the moment he came back from the city, which would be immediately after dinner.

The lady was happy that it was in her power to oblige the family, whom she much respected, or any of their connections, and readily presented the Major with the sum. She met the fate of all his other creditors, as he never after either called on her, or visited his lodgings.

Amongst the Russian anecdotes, we should have mentioned, that it is no secret to those who correspond with the mercantile part of that country, that Semple inveigled a great many people from different parts of the continent to some of those desarts and fortresses which border on the Crimea, to encourage the population of which, a bounty is allowed by government. These poor people being decoyed hither, with the view of a comfortable settlement, were landed without having any provision whatever made for them. They are said to have all perished, and that the agent who brought them from their own country put the bounty in his pocket. He abandoned the empire the moment this fact transpired.

Immediately on coming to England the last time (for he has frequently been upon the continent) he called on Mr. Southern, pretending the greatest intimacy with his brother in Russia. He said he had left

Peterf-

Peterſburgh in ſo much haſte, being intruſted with ſome important buſineſs of government, that he had not time to wait on that gentleman juſt on ſetting out for London. But he thought it his duty, on account of the friendſhip ſubſiſting between them, to take the earlieſt opportunity of acquainting him that his brother and family were well in Peterſburgh. Mr. Southern invited the Major to his table, where he dined with him ſeveral times.

As he called on him one day, he went into Mr. Stuart's, a perfumer, and ordered goods to the value of fifteen pounds. Theſe he obtained on the credit of his intimacy with Mr. Southern, which Mr. Stuart could have no doubt about, as he frequently had ſeen them together, and was perfectly acquainted with Mr. Southern's character and credit.

At Warrington, in Lancaſhire, he had nearly took in a gentleman of property, as great an adept in the art of keeping, as Semple has hitherto proved himſelf in that of getting.

While he was in the chief tavern of Warrington he made it his buſineſs to enquire into the character, fortune and connection of all the principal inhabitants. Mr. Bent, a rich merchant, and a bachelor, appeared to him the moſt likely perſon to ſupply him with caſh. He introduced himſelf to Mr. B. as a Colonel in the Ruſſian ſervice, on a viſit, to ſee his friends in England. He ſaid alſo he had got acquainted with a moſt beautiful young lady, whoſe fortune was immenſe, and was thus far on his way to Scotland,

to

to be married, as she was not yet of age. From motives of delicacy he wished to keep the transaction a secret from his friends, until it was accomplished. He found himself short of cash. He applied to him, as thinking him most likely to be acquainted with some of his friends, several of whom he mentioned. One of these it seemed lived a few miles distant from Warrington. Mr. Bent told the Major, that it would take up some little time before he could make up the sum. But as soon as it was completed he would send to the Major where he lodged. Bent instantly sent to the gentleman, whom the Major had mentioned among the list of his friends. The answer was, that they knew no such person. This being announced to the Major, (a word to the wife is enough) he marched off.

Notorious cheats, or, in smoother language, gentlemen who live by trick and cunning, are subject to have offences laid at their door of which they are *not* guilty; this is the case respecting a bill on Child, the banker, mentioned in this page of the last edition.

The gentleman who holds this bill has lately, by the Lord Mayor's permission, seen the Major in Newgate, and declares he is *not* the man.

Of a shoe-maker, at or near Egham, he (the Major) bespoke a pair of boots; the man knew his

his general character, and took the order with indifference; however, as he was determined not to
leave the boots without the money; and as they
were a common fize, he made them, and carried them home; when, to his furprife, he received the money the moment he had tried them
on. About three days after, the Major called
at the fhoemaker's houfe, and told him, he liked
the boots fo well, that he would have a dozen
pair made exactly like them, to take to America,
where he fhould go fhortly. He replied, " No,
" Major, that bait will not do at prefent, I know
" you; you have, indeed, deceived me once, (al-
" luding to his paying him unexpectedly) but it
" fhall be my fault if you do fo again." This
unexpected reply, and the difappointment, irritated
the Major fo much, that he ftruck the man with
his cane in his own fhop, and ran out as faft as
poffible; the fhoemaker overtook him, and with a
ftrap, which he had in his hand, made the Major's
fhoulders warm, till he took fhelter in a neighbouring houfe.

In giving an account of this extraordinary impoftor, it will not be amifs to inform the reader,
that he could not have reigned half the time he
did, if the people in general, whom he had rob-
bed, had not been frequently tempted to difcharge
him

him upon receiving the value of their goods; he always took care to have money about him for that purpose, when he found himself likely to be taken before a magistrate, or profecuted for fraud.

The Major lodged a fhort time at Nando's, in Fleet-ftreet, a very refpectable houfe, much frequented by country gentlemen as an hotel, and kept by Mr. Grange: here he borrowed cafh under various pretences, of almoft every gentleman whom he fat with; one in particular he agreed to accompany at five o'clock the next morning to Oxford in the ftage or poft-coach; but, as he was at fupper, recollected he had no cafh, and he had then no opportunity of applying to his banker, who was fhut up; the gentleman whom he was to travel with, rather than lofe his company, lent him ten pounds; but the Major thought proper to walk out about eleven o'clock that evening, and did not return before nine or ten o'clock next morning; his companion was confequently obliged to go alone, declaring he would pull the Major's nofe the next time he faw him. The Major hearing this, put on the appearance of courage, fwearing he would not fleep till he meafured fwords with the rafcal, and ordered a chaife directly for Oxford.

The chaife came to the door, the Major ftepped in, but went no nearer Oxford than Holborn; as foon as he arrived there, he ordered the boy to turn about, go over London Bridge, and proceed

Q

to

to Dartford, in his way to Dover, where he arrived
the next morning, and put up at the York Hotel.
Here he saw several servants, in a handsome livery;
he enquired of one of them who his master was;
the man replied, Sir Samson Gideon, who is
just arrived from the continent. The Major requested he would inform Sir Samson, a gentleman wished to pay his respects to him. The
servant observing the Major had the appearance
of what he stiled himself, delivered the message
to his master, who desired the stranger might
be admitted. After the usual salutations, Sir
Samson requested to know, what circumstance
he was indebted to, for the honor of the visit.
Here the Major put on the appearance of great
distress, and declared himself the most miserable
of men, having but the morning before *mortally
wounded* his man in a duel.—The quarrel, he said,
happened at Nando's Coffee-house, where his an-
tagonist lodged; they were both unhappily a little
heated with wine; and their seconds also, or the
unfortunate rencontre would not have taken place.
To add to his distress, he had not time to call at
his banker's, and was actually flying to the continent with only two or three guineas in his pocket.
Sir Samson immediately presented him with ten
pieces, wished him a safe voyage, and a speedy end
to his present embarrassment.

When

When Sir Samson arrived in town, he sent to
Nando's to enquire after the unfortunate man
who had been *mortally wounded*, and then difcovered the whole impofition.

A few days before he was apprehended, he introduced himſelf to Mr. Chapman, woollen-draper,
oppofite the New Church in the Strand, *as the
fon of Lord Semple;* obferving, that, as he had
furnifhed cloth, to clothe his father's regiment,
he would, being now returned to England, after a
long abfence abroad, deal with him, for fuch trifles
as he fhould want in future for himfelf and fervants. Mr. Chapman had really ferved Lord
Semple and the regiment, therefore had no doubt
of his being the man he had reported himfelf; he
thanked the Major for his intentions, and let him
have about eight pounds worth of cloth, for which
he took his note.

It is a queſtion among the gentlemen of the
law, whether this tranfaction is any more than a
debt. Some, however, are of opinion, that, as
he perfonated Lord Semple's fon, which it is notorious he is not, it is a fraud.

At Mr. Chapman's, in order, it was fuppofed,
to ingratiate himfelf, and obtain large credit, he
had ordered a parcel to be left, directed for himfelf. This parcel, when he was apprehended, was
delivered to the Lord Mayor, and found to contain the letters from Mr. Pitt, Dr. Pretyman, and

others,

others, which he had so frequently and advantage-
oufly difplayed before. Some time after he was
committed, he petitioned for thofe letters, as ufeful
in forming his defence; and his Lordfhip humanely
returned them.

He lodged a fhort time in Mitre Court, Fleet-
ftreet; during that period he employed Mr. Andrews, hair-dreffer, in Tanfield Court, in the Temple, to drefs him; on the day he agreed with Mr.
Andrews, he ordered him to come *himfelf* at four
o'clock, and not to fend one of his men, for he
was going to dine with Mr. Pitt, and muft therefore be dreffed in the beft manner.

Mr. Andrews kept his word, and, to his furprize,
found him fat down to an excellent dinner, which
had been juft fent from Joe's Coffee-houfe. Mr.
Andrews, while he waited in the room where
he was dining, could not help obferving, that he
underftood he was to have dined with Mr. Pitt.
The poor Major was quite confufed the moment
it was mentioned, and in a hefitating manner faid,
" God blefs me, fo I was, I had quite forgot."
Mr. Andrews fufpected him from that moment;
yet he had the adroitnefs to borrow fix guineas of
him that afternoon; and in a few days, for per-
fumes, curls, dreffing, and cafh, he difappeared,
about nine pounds in his debt. · Brown's and Joe's
coffee-houfes, which are both in the fame court,
had the honour to board him elegantly and *gratis*,
while he lodged there.

Of

Of Mr. Chambers, wine-merchant, in Craven-street, he borrowed seventeen guineas, under similar pretences with others which he had often used before.

Of Mr. Worboys, silver-smith, in Fleet-street, he obtained several small articles, and borrowed half a guinea in cash; he made other attempts, but could not succeed, as Mr. Worboys was upon his guard.

Notwithstanding the black and numerous list of frauds already exhibited against Major Semple, we may, with great attention to truth, assert, that this pamphlet has not exhibited the whole of his offences, either in magnitude or number, particularly in the northern parts of England.

He was at Leeds about two years since, and obtained a message from a young lady whom he danced with at a public ball, to her brother at Halifax: the lady happened to mention, that she was only on a visit at Leeds, and that her home was at Halifax, where she lived with a brother; this was excellent information for our Major; it was all he then wanted; he immediately replied, I am going upon a recruiting party to Halifax, and shall set out soon in the morning; if you have any letter or message to your brother, I will think myself honoured by your commands. The lady said, you may give my love to him, and inform him I intend to return home in about ten

days,

days, at the same time giving him her brother's address. He was now in his element; this message gave him a new opportunity of displaying his talents, and duping the unwary. The moment he arrived at Halifax, he introduced himself to the lady's brother, who entertained him in the most hospitable manner: after he found himself in possession of his host's good opinion, he began to open his masked-battery, and play upon his credulity; told him he was son of General Phillips; that he was himself Captain Philips, of the fifty-second regiment; that he had spent his money, and wanted fifty pounds to carry him on his recruiting journey, and enquired if he knew any army-agent in the town; the gentleman mentioned Mr. Breckon. He then took no further notice, but in a few hours after he completed his business, as will appear in the sequel of this anecdote. After dinner he walked out for a little fresh air, went to Mr. Breckon, and having introduced himself as Captain Philips in the manner before-mentioned, said he would be much obliged to him for fifty pounds, for which he would give his draft, payable in twenty-one days, upon his agent in London: he mentioned (in order to remove all suspicion) his intimacy with the lady before mentioned, and her brother, also her relations and friends at Leeds and Halifax, though, in fact, he knew nothing of any of them, except what he had learned of the brother in answer to

his

his questions concerning his family and friends; and, in order to lead him on, was very communicative respecting his own family, particularly his father's campaigns, and honourable death, in America.

In short, Mr. Breckon was, though a gentleman of experience in life, most completely thrown off his guard, and laying his usual prudence aside, advanced the money, taking his draft in the name of Philips, which turned out just as valuable as a slip of blank paper.

Neither Mr. Breckon, nor the gentleman through whom he gained his confidence, nor even his lovely sister, as he called her, ever saw him after.

At Durham, and at Darlington, he raised a few pounds between Mr. Richardson, senior, who kept an inn in the first place, and his son, who also kept an inn at the other. Here he was Major Sawyer.

He was arrested at Oxford, (see page twenty-nine,) for or about thirty pounds; when in the officer's house he wrote to Mrs. Semple, to raise the money necessary to discharge debt and costs, and she, forgiving the train of injuries which she had combated through his villanies, prevailed upon Baron Hompesch, whom he had before defrauded (see page 32.) to lend her the money, which he did. Mr. Mann, of Mitre Court, who has a large family, and keeps a little fruit-shop, was, on account of former proofs of fidelity, entrusted with the money, and received a guinea himself, for his expences and trouble in going and coming from Oxford. He liberated the Major, agreeable to his instructions, who, in return, *borrowed that very guinea of him*, which he never returned.

He tempted Mr. Feltham, who took him in the singular manner related in page 63, by offering
him

him the full amount of his debt, and 20 guineas beside; but he, with proper spirit, replied, " *The* " *crown of England shall not ransom you.*" He kept his word, and he deserves the thanks of the public, for preferring their benefit to his own private emolument. He was, however, first tried for robbing Mr. Lycett, a coach-maker; *vide* the Trial, page 138 to 152; and had he escaped conviction for that offence, Mr. Feltham's, and many other indictments, were prepared, in order, if possible, to bring this enemy of mankind to justice: there were no less than seven bills found against him by the GRAND JURY!!

We cannot close this account of Mr. Feltham's spirited conduct better than by inserting the follow-ing unanimous *vote of thanks, which has appeared in the Public-papers.*

The Guardians; or, Society for the protec-tion of trade against swindlers and sharpers.

At a quarterly general Meeting of this Society, held at the Mitre Tavern, Fleet-street, on the 29th of Sep-tember, 1786, it was unanimously resolved,

That the thanks of this Society be given to Mr. WIL-LIAM FELTHAM, of Fleet-street, hatter, for his vigilance and activity in apprehending and bringing to justice, *James George Semple,* commonly called *Major Semple.*

By order of the said meeting,

EDWARD S. FOSS, Sec.

At a subsequent meeting of the said society, they have, in addition, voted Mr. Feltham a piece of plate.

When

When he was removed from the Compter to
Newgate, and the turnkey was *dreſſing* the Major
with an ornament to his ſilk ſtockings, he begged
that a gentleman of his character and importance might not be ſo diſgraced. That he was
treated like a gentleman at the former priſon,
where he had behaved himſelf like a gentleman
alſo, having ſlipped five guineas into the turnkey's hand.

This, however, proved a falſehood, inſtead
of having behaved himſelf like a gentleman, he
had left the Compter a few ſhillings in the debt
of a poor old waſherwoman.

R   THE

THE

Trial of James George Semple,

alias Harrold, &c. &c.

ON Saturday the fecond of September 1786,
the PRISONER was put to the bar, and
arraigned before Mr. Juftice Gould and the
Recorder of London. The indictment ftated, that
James George Semple, otherwife Harrold, otherwife Kennedy, did on the firft day of September,
1785, of Richard Lycett, coachmaker, one chaife,
commonly called a poft-chaife, of the value of
fifty pounds, *felonioufly fteal, take, and carry away*
againft the peace, &c.

The *alias dictus* having been added, in this indictment, to the fubftantive name, and no other
objection being made thereto, Mr. Lycett was
called, who fwore

That he was a coachmaker in Whitechapel, and
let out carriages for hire; and that he knew the
prifoner perfectly well. That on the firft day
of September, in the year 1785, the prifoner
came to his houfe, and hired a poft-chaife for three
weeks or a month, for which he was to pay five
fhillings per day; that the prifoner had the carriage delivered to his order, which carriage Mr.
Lycett never had the pleafure of feeing again, nor
the

the prifoner, till Mr. Lycett faw him in confinement in the Poultry Compter.

Mr. Lycett further fwore, that the prifoner
came to him recommended from the Saracen's-
Head, Aldgate, where he then lodged. That he
had hired a carriage of him once before; which
was on the 10th of July preceding, for fix fhillings
a day, which he returned on the fixteenth, and
paid for.

That the carriage which the prifoner had the
fecond time, and for which he then ftood indicted,
was by the prifoner's direction altered, by having
piftol holfters put to it, and a net to the roof,
with the platform reduced to the fize of the Major's
trunk.

He alfo fwore, that the prifoner told him that
the carriage was wanted for a tour to the north;
that it was delivered on the fame day to a fervant
of Mr. Bolton's, John Deacon, who keeps the
Saracen's-Head Inn; that it was three weeks or a
month for which it was hired, and that it was to
be returned in that time.

That he had never heard from him afterwards;
that he was fure the prifoner at the bar was the fame
perfon, and had not the leaft doubt of it. That
there was no agreement to fell the chaife, or to keep
it longer than three or four weeks, and then pay
fifty-two guineas for it; but that the prifoner faid,
' Suppofe I fhould have a mind to buy it, what

' would

' would it be worth?' to which Mr. Lycett replied, ' About fifty-two guineas;' but that there
was a fale, either abfolutely or conditionally, Mr.
Lycett pofitively denied.

He added alfo, that, unfortunately for him,
this was not the chaife the prifoner had firft fpoke
about; the chaife he obtained was almoft a new
one; the other, which the prifoner had before,
and which he had then let to a gentleman for
three or four days, was an old one.

' The Recorder of London, who tried the prifoner, then put the following queftions to Mr.
Lycett.

Did you part with the chaife with any expecta-
tion of the prifoner's being a purchafer? to which
Mr. Lycett replied, By no means.

The evident meaning of the above queftion was,
to fhew what was in the contemplation of the
parties at the actual time of the prifoner's hiring
the carriage; for if there had been any idea of a
purchafe, the felony would have been inftantly reduced to a fimple debt.

Mr. Lycett then underwent a very long and
critical crofs examination from Mr. Garrow, who
was concerned for the prifoner as his counfel.

Mr. Garrow feemed anxious to bring him to
acknowledge that he meant to have made it only
a debt. This, however, Mr. Lycett flatly denied.
His evidence afforded much entertainment to the
court from the confiftency of his ftory, his un-
embarraffed

embarraffed attention to what he was about, and particularly by the fmartnefs of his replies.

He was afked who was concerned in the profecution, and whether it did not originate at the inftigation of Mr. Feltham, hatter, in Fleet-ftreet.

Mr. Lycett acknowledged his obligations to Mr. Feltham for his advice; but added, that he believed his own pocket would be faddled with, and was able to defray, all the expences of the profecution.

Well but, faid Mr. Garrow, how did the prifoner demean himfelf? Did he go about the bufinefs as you and I would have done?

O no, faid the witnefs, his addrefs is very different, I affure you. He is not fo *rough*; he is a gentleman; his manners are perfectly *polifhed*.

Mr. Lycett produced his book, at the réqueft of the counfel; when it appeared that the prifoner had obtained the firft chaife under the name of Major Harrold.

It appeared alfo, that after the name Harrold, there had been an erafure, on which erafure ftood the name of Semple; and being interrogated ftrictly on this point, Mr. Lycett faid that he put down every name which he had heard the prifoner had went by; that there were three or four names at times put down, one of which had been the Marquis of Carmarthen; and that he put every name down till he had got the right one, which he difcovered about three quarters of a year
ago,

ago, at a Mr. Sadgrove's, a hair-dreſſer, at Knightſbridge, with whom the priſoner had lodged.

He was then aſked, if he had not called the priſoner a damned ſcoundrel, and ſaid that he would arreſt him for 5ol. The former part of the queſtion Mr. Lycett readily acknowledged, but poſitively denied the latter.

Mr. Lycett, in his croſs examination, further ſaid, that he never gave the priſoner a bill of 5ol. for the chaiſe, nor ever ſued out any writ againſt him: that his ſervant, John Marchant, delivered the chaiſe to Deacon: that the priſoner behaved in a fine flouriſhing and poliſhed manner; and that he ſhould have reſted very happy if the carriage had been ever returned. He denied ever receiving a bank-note of ten pounds in part of the carriage; and ſaid that his own pocket ſuffered for the proſecution; however, he thought it right to puniſh ſuch offenders.

Mr. Garrow then made an ingenious ſuppoſition, that where the eraſure ſtood in the book, there had been wrote " or to pay fifty guineas;" but this Mr. Lycett poſitively denied.

John Marchant, apprentice to Mr. Lycett, proved delivering the carriage to Deacon: and Deacon proved fetching it away from Mr. Lycett's. But although it appeared that Deacon had drove the priſoner once to Barnet and back, and took him up at Sadgrove's in Knightſbridge, and drove him to Uxbridge, from thence to the Duke of Portland's at Bulſtrode and back to town, yet

this

this witnefs could not fwear to the prifoner. On
his firft ftanding up to give his evidence, he defired to know who was to pay him for his trouble
and lofs of time; for which he was feverely repri-
manded by the court.

Mr. Bolton proved that the prifoner had been a
cuftomer of his in the name of Harrold; that he
went with him to Lycett's when the carriage was
hired; and that he knew nothing of any bargain
but that of hiring.

Mr. Silvefter, who was for the profecutor, being
but juft come into court, afked Mr. Bolton, If the
carriage was purchafed or hired? To which Mr.
Bolton replied, Hired.

The evidence being clofed, Mr. Garrow addreffed the court in a very long fpeech, to fhew
caufe why the prifoner fhould not be put on his
defence, as the fact ftated to the court made it
only a debt, and not a felony.

He cited many cafes, or rather ingenioufly conftrued many cafes, in a way contrary to their legal
conftructions; and blended the fact of hiring with
the fuppofed conditional purchafe, on which he
argued a confiderable while.

He begged leave to call the attention of the
court to fuch particular circumftances in the cafe
of his client, as he trufted would render all defence
on his part unneceffary. The tranfaction, in his
opinion, had all the requifites of a bargain between
one man with another. Taking up the matter on
this ground, he produced a variety of cafes to
eftablifh

establish this proposition, that as there appeared to him a bargain or agreement between the parties, Major Semple was chargeable only with having failed in fulfilling this part of the contract. The consequence was, that he could have redress by a recovery of his property in a civil suit. This was the jet of his argument; and he contended that it would rest with the Court to determine what the real nature of the fact or transaction between his client and Mr. Lycett was; and if they admitted with him the reality of a contract, he was satisfied in his own mind, that it was impossible that the case before the court could warrant a felonious charge.

The Recorder here stopped Mr. Garrow, and desired him to confine his argument to the hiring, as the purchase was denied, and said it was the province of the Jury to determine what the contract was. Judge Gould entirely coincided with the Recorder.

Mr. Garrow then argued simply on the hiring contract, and contended it was no felony.

Mr. Agar said a few words on the same side as Mr. Garrow, and called the prosecution an extraordinary conversion of a mere Westminster-Hall business to the bar of the Old Bailey.

He owned that he did not feel the force of the argument from the cases which had been quoted. He thought them inapplicable, and presumed the reasoning they were intended to support would be deemed inconclusive. He admitted the contract was

was not fully proved, and argued on the fuppofition that there was none, that it was only a
hiring fimply, and that it was a hire for a fpecific
time. But he defired the court, and particularly
the Jury, to beware of the confequence of pro-
nouncing his client guilty, becaufe he had not
delivered to Mr. Lycett his property within a certain time. He denied that there was any law
exifting, by which one man could charge another
felonioufly for not keeping his time to a day : and
where could the line be drawn? No limitation of
time whatever could conftitute felony by the laws
of England. He therefore thought his client's cafe
would bear him out on thefe principles, even fup-
pofing he could produce no exculpatory evidence.

Mr. Silvefter was going to reply, when the Recorder ftopped him, and faid he need not give
himfelf any trouble on the fubject, becaufe if the
Jury believed the evidence, there was no queftion
of law. He was joined in opinion by Judge
Gould, who thought the cafe fully within the late
adjucations. The opinion of counfel being thus
over-ruled, the prifoner was called upon for what
he had to fay in his own behalf, and addreffed the
court as follows:

THE PRISONER'S DEFENCE.

He informed the court, that while he lodged at
the Saracen's-Head, he had occafion to hire a carriage. There being none at the inn where he was,

to his mind, he was recommended to Mr. Lycett, from whom he hired one for seven days, as it was marked or entered in Mr. Lycett's book. Not long subsequent to this transaction, he bought a carriage from Mr. Licet at 50l. This he had upon trial. If it suited him he was to pay for it a twelvemonth afterwards; if not it was to be charged to him at 5s. per day. Mr. Lycett, however, alledging that altering the chaise for his accommodation had cost him a good deal of extra charges; and agreeing to defray these, Mr. Lycett presented him with a bill of about 6l. The prisoner then gave him a 10l. bank-note.

This was the substance of the prisoner's defence, which was not uttered in a manner that did much honour either to his education, his acknowledged abilities, or his appearance.

Mr. Lycett being asked about the 10l. note, said, The Major had flourished his hand about in his pockets, and jingled some money, but he never saw either cash or notes.

WITNESSES FOR THE PRISONER.

Mr. James Sadgrove was called, and swore that Mr. Lycett had told him he had let Major Harrold a post-chaise on trial, and that, if he liked it, he was to give him fifty-two guineas for it. Sadgrove acknowledged, on his cross examination, that some gentlemen had been with him from the prisoner.

Mr.

Mr. Lycett moſt poſitively denied any ſuch converſation; but owned that, not being a lawyer, he
could not tell whether or no, if he could have then
found the Major, he ſhould not have arreſted him

John Bowes, a hackney-coachman, was called to
know, if ever he had heard any converſation
between the priſoner and Mr. Lycett about the
chaiſe. He had driven the priſoner ſeveral times
to Mr. Lycett's, but never followed him into the
houſe or ſhop; and therefore heard no converſation.

· The Recorder, with that impartiality and fair-
eſs which has ever diſtinguiſhed his judicial character, and with a diſcrimination which reflects
equal merit on his abilities, ſummed up the evidence, and ſtated every part of it for and againſt
the proſecution, with great candour and exactneſs,
in which he replied to the objections urged by the
priſoner's counſel. · He denied that there was any
thing like a contract for a purchaſe proved.' So
that there was not the leaſt foundation for any rea-
ſoning on that ſuppoſition. ' There was in his opinion, yet leſs weight, if poſſible, in the argument
urged by Mr. Agar; for it ſtruck him as fairly
and completely made out in the caſe that the hiring
which had taken place was no more than a pre-
text made uſe of by the priſoner for getting poſſeſſion of Mr. Lycett's property, that he might
convert it to his own purpoſes. The hiring a chaiſe
before, and honourably paying the debt incurred by
that means, carrying on theſe tranſactions under a

fictitious

fictitious name, and never having to this moment
produced the carriage, were circumstances which
shewed that the property had been obtained with a
felonious intent. That the chaise was not hired
with any view either to return it, or pay for it,
and that the prisoner appeared to have no other object in what he did, than to realize whatever the
chaise could fetch for his own use. The simple,
question therefore on which the Jury were to decide,
was the nature of the transaction between Mr.
Lycett and the prisoner; and this opinion, he said,
met the concurrence of the first crown law authority, Judge Gould. If they thought he had really
hired the chaise with a view to restore it, and
pay for the time it was in his service, though from
necessity he had disposed of it, however such an
action might be condemned or punished as a breach
of trust, the law would not recognize it as felonious,
But if, on the contrary, they thought from the evidence which had been produced, that the hiring
was not *bona fide* on the prisoner's part, or, in
short, that they could not clear him of an intention
to possess himself of this property, he could assure
them there was no law against their bringing him
in GUILTY.

The Jury, after consulting among themselves for
the space of ten minutes, gave in their verdict—
Guilty.

The Recorder then asked them, Whether they
founded their verdict on the evidence given by
Mr.

Mr. Lycett, or that of Sadgrove; in other words, said he, Do you believe Mr. Lycett or Sadgrove? To which they replied, Mr. Lycett; when the Recorder obferved, he was exactly of their opinion.

And thus ended the trial of a genius who has excited as much curiofity as his depredations have caufed alarm; and for one of which the fentence of the law condemns him to tranfportation for feven years.

A MOTION FOR DEFERRING JUDGMENT, IN THE CASE OF MAJOR SEMPLE, AT THE OLD BAILEY, ON THURSDAY, SEPT. 7.

MAJOR James George Semple being ordered to make his appearance at the bar, and the clerk having announced to him the nature of his crime, and the verdict of the Jury, demanded of him, whether he had any reafons to adduce why the fentence of death* ought not immediately to be pronounced.

Mr. Garrow then addreffed himfelf to the bench. He acknowledged the integrity and ability of the judge, who had tried his client in very handfome and becoming terms. He trufted, what he had now to fay would not be imputed to any other principle than his fincere defire of doing juftice to his client. He ftood in circumftances peculiarly diftreffing and unfortunate. It was natural, thus fituated, for him, like every one who had any value for the bleffings of exiftence, to deprecate, or if poffible prevent, the augmentation of that preffure

of

---

* The offence being within the benefit of clergy, the prifoner in fingle felonies is allowed to plead it.

Before culprits met with this indulgence, the above queftion was put; and, even in clergyable offences it is ftill afked.

of mifery with which it was his deftiny to grapple, by having recourfe to all poffible expedients. This he conceived would apologize for the unhappy prifoner at the bar, and at the fame time for the part which it was his own lot now to act in his favour. He was, indeed, folicitous to defeat any prejudice which might arife in the breaft of the court againft the motion which, with all humility, he was now to make.

It was, That judgment in the cafe of Major James George Semple, who had been adjudged by the verdict—Guilty of felony, fhould be poftponed until next feffion.

He owned this motion did not originate with him; he was urged to fuggeft it in court by others, who thought the decifion on the cafe of his client afforded ground for it.

The reafons on which that opinion was founded were, that the facts proved were fimple and deftitute of thofe circumftances which conftituted felony. He quoted feveral cafes in fupport of that pofition. He denied that on the face of the cafe there was any thing to warrant the idea of a felonious intention. All that had been proved was the fingle tranfaction of hiring a chaife. The prifoner was not profecuted for not returning the goods, but that he took poffeffion of them with a felonious intent.

He would affert, with the greateft poffible deference for the opinion of the court, that fuch a verdict was not authenticated by the evidence which had been produced. It was on this fingle ground he prefumed at this time to trouble the court, and to befeech his lordfhip in behalf of the unhappy prifoner, that judgment in his cafe fhould be deferred until next feffion.

Mr. Agar rofe to fupport the motion, or rather requeft, made by his learned brother. He was in hopes that his motives in this bufinefs would bear no other conftruction than an honeft folicitude to urge

urge every plea in favour of his unhappy client, which the cafe would admit. Mr. Agar alfo had recourfe to feveral cafes, and endeavoured to fhew that the prefent one was altogether new, and totally diftinct from any thing which had occurred within the practice of modern times. It was a fact which all men converfant with the laws of the country knew, that fraud was a crime not only well defined and generally underftood, but a fpecial act of parliament had afcertained its nature, and determined its punifhment. This offence therefore was fpecifically provided againft. Why then inftitute precedents, which, in his mind, had a tendency to confound thofe things which were already fo perfectly diftinct; and indeed if the law, as adminiftered in the cafe of the prifoner, was to be confidered as eftablifhed, the crime of fraud was from that moment annihilated. There could be no fuch thing. Hiring, when the goods poffeffed by that means were not inftantly returned, would henceforth be deemed intentional felony.

Mr. Recorder faid, he was happy in having tried the prifoner in the prefence of one of the beft Crown lawyers in the kingdom*, who, fortunately, that day fat the whole time upon the bench. In the opinions which he then ftated, the learned judge had uniformly agreed with him. He did not well underftand the fhape which the bufinefs had now affumed. Merely poftponing judgment could not, fo far as his difcernment went, in any degree whatever ferve the prifoner. He was never more fatisfied in his own mind with the law, as applied to any cafe, than in this. The felonious intention was the firft circumftance in the fact on which the prifoner had been tried, that muft ftrike every perfon of common fenfe who took the matter into one moment's confideration. The verdict of the jury, in like manner, moft perfectly coincided with the idea of what he

* Mr. Juftice Gould.

he conceived to be their duty, from the moſt im-
partial view of the evidence as it lay completely
before them. But, however, it was very well
known the manner of redreſs in the priſoner's contemplation could not be obtained here. The court
was not competent to make any inquiry ſubſequent
to the verdict of jury. It was the province of his
Majeſty alone to afford ſuch relief as in his royal
wiſdom he might think neceſſary for ſoftening the
ſeverity of the law in the caſe of individuals.

Major Semple ſtated, that he only craved time
of the court for the purpoſe of proſecuting ſuch as
had perjured themſelves in their evidences againſt
him.

His ſentence.

Mr. Recorder then addreſſed himſelf to the priſoner, whom he cautioned againſt imagining that
the genteel accompliſhments which he poſſeſſed
were any mitigation of the offence, for a verdict of
a jury of his countrymen had pronounced him guilty.
He ought to have known better, and therefore de-
ſerved exemplary puniſhment. This was the opinion
of the court. It was his duty now to pronounce the
ſentence of the law upon him for the offence of
which he had been found guilty; and that was,
That he ſhould be tranſported for ſeven years beyond the ſeas to wherever his Majeſty, with the advice of his privy council, might judge it proper to
ſend him.

SINCE

Since the Publication of the SIXTH EDITION
OF THESE MEMOIRS, the following circumstances have come to the Editor's know-
lege, from very respectable authority.

ABOUT the year 1778 the Major is supposed to
have made his first appearance as a Soldier, at the
Thatched-House Tavern, in St. James's Street,
where he dined with a respectable company. He
said he was the Hon. Mr. Semple, *Son of Lord
Semple*, just returned from America; He also
added, he had been fighting for his Country, as
a Volunteer, with other young. gentlemen of
spirit, who formed themselves into a regiment
distinguished by the appellation of THE LOYAL
AMERICAN VOLUNTEERS. He was then, according to his own account, twenty-three years old,
a handsome figure, and elegantly dressed, in a
kind of hussar uniform, a very light gun, and
neat side-arms, particularly a small bayonet,
which he had acquired the art of throwing from

T   his

his hand ſe diſtance of ſix or eight yards, with
great exctneſs, ſo as to hit a ſmall card repeatedly Here he related his adventures with
great ſvacity, and engaged the attention of the
comſany much;—the concluſion, to be ſure,
was rather ſerious and intereſting.

He obſerved that, notwithſtanding he poſſeſſed
ſuch a flow of ſpirits, he was a very unhappy
man at that very inſtant; for, having ſome words
the night before with a gentleman of the Guards,
a Lieutenant Davis, who frequented the York
Coffee-houſe, he found it impoſſible *to preſerve
his honour,* but by calling him out; which he
had done, with great reluctance, that morning,
and left him wounded, (ſuppoſed mortally) in
Hyde-Park, where they fought.

Another embarraſſing circumſtance was, how
he could reach the Continent without money?
for, unluckily, he had but fifteen ſhillings in his
pocket; however, he had a very good bill upon a
gentleman of known fortune in the city, and added,
he would be obliged to any of the company who,
conſidering the peculiarity of his ſituation, would
immediately advance the caſh for it.

Whether they doubted his tale, or had not the
money (about forty pounds) it is not now eaſy
to aſcertain, but it is certain he did not then ſucceed in his principal object, which was the negociation of this bill.

One of the company, Mr. G——r, a ſurgeon,
who was going to ſpend his evening at the Globe
Tavern

Tavern in Fleet-ſtreet, invited Mr. Semple to meet him there; where, perhaps, he might ſucceed better.—Mr. G. really believed the whole of his ſtory, and therefore endeavoured to ſerve him from the beſt of motives—humanity.

Semple was punctual to the appointment, where he recounted his adventures, as before; exerciſed the bayonet with great dexterity, and raiſed the attention and admiration of all preſent;—but the bill ſtill continued in his poſſeſſion. He had drawn the long bow ſo often during that evening's converſation, that thoſe troubleſome intruders, called DOUBTS, had damped their inclination to ſupply his purſe, notwithſtanding his neceſſities were ſo very preſſing. Mr. Semple ſlept that night at the Swan with two Necks, in Lad-lane, as he pretended, to evade all enquiry or ſearch that might be made after him by the officers of juſtice.

However, Mr. G——r, the next morning, ſent to the York Coffee-houſe, to enquire after Lieut. Davis, when the whole deception came out, as many others of a ſimilar nature have, ſince that period.

The Major at this time began to diſplay the contemptible profeſſion of a Raſcal; he found theſe ſort of duels were fought without danger, yet in his own imagination raiſed wonder, and created reſpect: theſe honourable rencounters likewiſe anſwered another purpoſe; they often have, as appears in theſe adventures, by making favourable
impreſſions,

impreffions, expanded the heart;—the operations of that index to the mind have an amazing effect upon the purfe.

The neceffit of flying to the Continent unprepared for the expences of a journey, created in his deluded companions an inclination to remove his wants, either by lending him an immediate fupply in cafh, or difcounting a fwindling bill. His pur-pofe was anfwered either way and by one method or the other he generally fucceeded: experience has, however, taught him that fuch infamous modes of acquiring a fubfiftance, can be but of fhort duration; and though the wings of Juftice are fometimes formed of lead, and therefore but flow in their motion, her fingers are made of iron, with which fhe holds faft thofe who have dared to treat her precepts with contempt.

At Birmingham he introduced himfelf to Mr. Clay, japanner to His Majefty, faw all his works, and entertained him with a defcription of the fimi-lar manufactories which he had feen abroad. After he had obtained complete poffeffion of his good opinion, he made an apology for the liberty he was going to take; he believed he fhould be obliged to afk credit of his Landlady, Mrs. Lloyd, at the Hen and Chickens, where he had been three or four days, till he returned, unlefs he (Mr. Clay) would affift him with ten guineas, for which he would give his draught on his banker in London. This fum Mr. C. immediately ad-vanced, and took his draught in exchange.

He then went to Meff. Richards and Co. in the fame Town, and purchafed twenty pounds worth of different toys and trinkets, for which he gave
another

another draught on London; then ordered a p\
chaife from a different ftreet than that in whi\
he had lodged, and drove to Bridgenorth, in hi\
way to Shrewfbury: on that, or the next day,
Mr. Clay faw, in the London papers, the Major's
perfon particularly defcribed, with a reward for
apprehending him: he inftantly applied to Mrs.
Lloyd, and found he had taken French leave of
her, without difcharging his bill, or returning
five guineas which he had borrowed of her.
Meff. Richards, who had fold him the toys, fent
a meffenger after him, by whom he was overtaken
at Bridgenorth; and where he recovered all the
goods: but Mr. Clay and Mrs. Lloyd never
faw the Major, or their money, fince. Meff.
Richards's meffenger would have detained him,
in confequence of the reward offered in the London
papers, which Mr. Clay had informed him of;
but the Magiftrate declined committing him till
his identity could be proved, by fending to London.—[It is to be much lamented that our Lord
Lieutenants are fo negligent in the appointment
of Magiftrates, as fome of them are too ignorant
to fill even the moft trifling offices.]—He played
feveral fimilar tricks at Shrewfbury, but the Editor is not yet in poffeffion of them.

We have before mentioned Mr. Gapper, of the
Temple, (fee page 81): fince the laft edition of
thefe Memoirs was printed, our information
refpecting that Gentleman has been extended.—
The Major called upon him one morning in the
Temple, and, after converfing with him about
a pretended law-fuit, obferving he was dreffed,
and going out, faid, in his eafy, familiar manner,
"Gapper,

pper, which way are you going?" he re-
d, " To a Lady's near Bedford-square."
Come, that's lucky; I am going that way also,
and my carriage shall set you down."—As soon as
they arrived, the Major enquired how long he
would stay? Mr. G. replied, " Not above three
quarters of an hour."—" Oh, very well; in all
probability I shall be able to return by that time,
and will call and take you back." Mr. G. bowed;
the Major returned before the time, and immediately, without sending his name, ran up stairs,
and, introducing himself to the Lady, made an
apology for returning so soon, which, he added,
was owing to the person he called upon being
gone into the country. In a short time Mr. G.
and he returned to the Temple, as proposed.—
Has the Reader yet discovered the Major's views
in this business? I should rather suppose, after
reading so many anecdotes of his ingenuity, he
has; however, to remove all doubts, be it known,
he had now a new object to dissemble with, and
he delayed the business but a short time; for the
very next morning he paid his respects to the Lady,
apologised, as usual, for the liberty he was about
to take, but he was most awkwardly situated: he
had placed his coach-horses and carriage in the
neighbourhood, for a few days, and was now
going to take them away; he had come from his
lodgings without any money in his pocket, except
a fifty pound bill, which the people at the livery
stable could not change; that he could not think
of taking away his horses, though they had offered
it, without paying the man; and would therefore
be much obliged to the Lady for five guineas,
which

which he would punctually return that evening, or
the next morning. It is, I suppose, unneceffary
to inform the Reader, that the Major obferved his
ufual and regular line of conduct, by never troubling her with a vifit, or meffenger, afterwards:
however, when Mr. Gapper had occafion to wait
upon the Lady again, fhe enquired after his friend,
and mentioned the circumftance, which brought
forward an inveftigation no way complimentary to
the Major's veracity or honour.

F I N I S.

BOOKS printed for G. KEARSLEY.

arranged in Chronological Order: also a short Account of his Life; and the Monody on his Death, written by Mr. SHERIDAN, and spoken by Mrs. YATES, of Drury-Lane Theatre. In two volumes. Price 7s. in Boards.

The POETICAL WORKS of SAMUEL JOHN-SON, LL. D. containing, London, a Satire.—The Vanity of Human Wishes.—Irene, a Tragedy.—The Winter's Walk.—Stella in Mourning.—The Midsummer's Wish.—An Evening Ode to Stella.—Vanity of Wealth.—The Natural Beauty.—Translation of Pope's Messiah into Latin; and sundry others. Price 2s. 6d.

ESSAYS on SUICIDE, and the IMMORTALITY of the SOUL; ascribed to the late DAVID HUME, Esq. With REMARKS, intended as an Antidote to the Poison contained in these Performances, by the Editor.

To which are added,

Two LETTERS on SUICIDE, from ROUSSEAU's ELOISA. Price 3s. 6d. sewed.

⁎ These Essays have been, for some Time, clandestinely circulated at a very extravagant Price, without any Comment.—This mysterious Mode of Sale, by rendring them an Object of Request, has considerably enhanced their Value.—The Notes which accompany and improve this Edition, are written by a Clergyman of the Church of England, and will appear to every serious Reader of Taste and Discernment, a satisfactory Answer to every thing exceptionable in the Text.

Printed in the United States
148244LV00006B/3/A